Family Bible Study

THE
Herschel
HOBBS
COMMENTARY

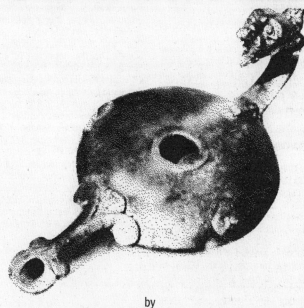

by

Robert J. Dean

WINTER 2001-02
Volume 2, Number 2

ROSS H. McLAREN
Biblical Studies Specialist

Carolyn Gregory
Production Specialist

Stephen Smith
Graphic Designer

Frankie Churchwell
Carla Dickerson
Technical Specialists

Send questions/comments to
  Ross H. McLaren, editor
  127 9th Ave., North
  Nashville, TN 37234-0175
  Email: HHobbsComm@lifeway.com

Management Personnel

Louis B. Hanks, *Acting Director*
Adult Sunday School Ministry Department
Louis B. Hanks, *Associate Director*
Sunday School Group
BILL L. TAYLOR, *Director*
Sunday School Group

ACKNOWLEDGMENTS.–We believe the Bible has God for its author; salvation for its end; and truth, without any mixture of error, for its matter and that all Scripture is totally true and trustworthy. The 2000 statement of *The Baptist Faith and Message* is our doctrinal guideline.

Unless otherwise indicated, all Scripture quotations are from the *King James Version.* This translation is available in a Holman Bible and can be ordered through LifeWay Christian Stores. Scripture quotations identified as CEV are from the *Contemporary English Version.* Copyright © American Bible Society 1991, 1992. Used by permission. Quotations marked HCSB have been taken from the *Holman Christian Standard Bible,* © Copyright 2000 by Broadman & Holman Publishers. Used by permission. This translation is available in a Holman Bible and can be ordered through LifeWay Christian Stores. Passages marked NASB are from the *New American Standard Bible: 1995 Update.* © The Lockman Foundation, 1960, 1962, 1963, 1968, 1971, 1972, 1973, 1975, 1977, 1995. Used by permission. This translation is available in a Holman Bible and can be ordered through LifeWay Christian Stores. Quotations marked NEB are from *The New English Bible.* Copyright © The Delegates of the Oxford University Press and the Syndics of the Cambridge University Press, 1961, 1970. Reprinted by permission. Quotations marked NIV are from the *Holy Bible, New International Version,* copyright © 1973, 1978, 1984 by International Bible Society (NIVmg. = NIV margin). This translation is available in a Holman Bible and can be ordered through Lifeway Christian Stores. Quotations marked NKJV are from the *New King James Version.* Copyright © 1979, 1980, 1982. Thomas Nelson, Inc., Publishers. Reprinted with permission. This translation is available in a Holman Bible and can be ordered through Lifeway Christian Stores. Quotations marked NRSV are from the *New Revised Standard Version of the Bible,* copyright © 1989 by the Division of Christian Education of the National Council of the Churches of Christ in the United States of America. Used by permission. All rights reserved. Quotations marked REB are from *The Revised English Bible.* Copyright © Oxford University Press and Cambridge University Press, 1989. Reprinted by permission.

The Herschel Hobbs Commentary (ISSN 0191-4219), *Family Bible Study*, is published quarterly for adult teachers and members using the Family Bible Study series by LifeWay Christian Resources of the Southern Baptist Convention, 127 Ninth Avenue, North, Nashville, Tennessee 37234, Gene Mims, President, LifeWay Church Resources, a division of LifeWay Christian Resources; James T. Draper, Jr., President, Ted Warren, Executive Vice-President, LifeWay Christian Resources; Bill L. Taylor, Director, Sunday School Group. © Copyright 2001 LifeWay Christian Resources of the Southern Baptist Convention. All rights reserved. Single subscription to individual address, $20.95 per year. If you need help with an order, WRITE LifeWay Church Resources Customer Service, 127 Ninth Avenue North, Nashville, Tennessee 37234-0113; For subscriptions, FAX (615) 251-5818 or EMAIL subscribe@lifeway.com. For bulk shipments mailed quarterly to one address, FAX (615) 251-5933 or EMAIL CustomerService@lifeway.com. Order ONLINE at www.lifeway.com. Mail address changes to: *The Herschel Hobbs Commentary, Family Bible Study,* 127 Ninth Avenue, North, Nashville, TN 37234-0113.

Dedicated to the memory of

Harry M. Piland

(August 23, 1928—May 24, 2001).

Minister of education in several churches,

Director of the Sunday School Division,

LifeWay Christian Resources, 1978—1994.

Loved by family, friends, and co-workers.

Appreciated by all who were touched

by his life and ministry.

Contents

Contents

Study Theme

Christmas: Celebrating Jesus' Birth

Some people have a cynical attitude toward Christmas. They consider it all a farce. One reason for this cynicism is the failure of the so-called Christmas spirit to extend beyond the season.

Christmas is over. Uncork your ambition!
Back to the battle! Come on, competition![1]

We cannot deny that this statement accurately depicts how some people confine their so-called "Christmas spirit" to one day or one season. Often these same people fail to celebrate Christmas in a Christian way. The Christian way focuses on Jesus and carries over to all the year.

This five-session study focuses on the birth of Jesus and the biblical truths that are prominent in the Christmas message. The purpose of this study is to help each of us to understand the meaning and message of Christmas and celebrate Jesus' birth properly.

The five sessions are designed to help you

• Celebrate Christmas by focusing on God's provision of redemption (week of Dec. 2, based on Gal. 3:26–4:7)

• Have the hope that God gives (week of Dec. 9, based on Rom. 15:1-13)

• Consistently keep Jesus' birth at the center of your celebration of Christmas (week of Dec. 16, based on Luke 2:4-20)

• Demonstrate God's kind of love in practical, concrete ways (week of Dec. 23, based on John 3:16 and 1 John 3:11-24)

• Make Jesus most important in your life (week of Dec. 30, based on Phil. 3:1-14)

Most of the Bible passages are not ones we usually use at the Christmas season. The exceptions are Galatians 4:4-5; John 3:16; and Luke 2:4-20. These are so familiar that people need to take a fresh look at the meaning and application of these Scriptures. At first sight the other Focal Passages may not appear to focus on Christmas; however, each focuses on some theme that is appropriate to the season.

[1]Franklin P. Adams, "For the Other 364 Days," in *American Quotations*, ed. by Gorton Carruth and Eugene Ehrlich [New York: Wing Books, 1994], 132.

THE MESSAGE OF CHRISTMAS

Background Passage: Galatians 3:26–4:20
Focal Passage: Galatians 3:26–4:7
Key Verses: Galatians 4:4-5

❖ *Significance of the Lesson*

• The *Theme* of this lesson is that Christmas is the celebration of Jesus' coming into the world—"born of a woman" (Gal. 4:4)—to redeem people from their sins.

• The *Life Question* addressed by this lesson is, What's to celebrate at Christmas?

• The *Biblical Truth* is that at exactly the right time, God sent His Son to redeem people from their sins.

• The *Life Impact* is to help you celebrate Christmas by focusing on God's provision of redemption.

Christmas and Redemption

In the secular worldview, Christmas is only a holiday. Many restrict their idea of its religious meaning to manger scenes. They fail to see the redemptive purpose of Jesus' coming into the world. In fact, redemption from sin is not a part of their concern at any season.

In the biblical worldview, the emphasis is on God's sending His Son into the world to redeem us as sinners. God sent His Son in His own time and way. Jesus was born of a virgin, but truly born. The unique Son of God came so that those who believe in Him might be redeemed from sin, made sons of God, and receive His Spirit.

Paul's Letter to the Galatians

Galatians is Paul's most emotional letter. In his other letters, the apostle followed his greeting with words of affirmation for the readers. However, in this letter he moved quickly to strong words of rebuke (1:6-9). Paul probably had started the churches in Galatia during his first missionary journey. After he left, false teachers (Judaizers) followed Paul and undermined the gospel of salvation by grace through faith, substituting a message of faith plus circumcision and keeping the law. Paul tolerated people who preached the true gospel even from wrong motives (Phil. 1:15-18); however, he reacted strongly against anyone who preached a false gospel. Thus he wrote the Letter to the Galatians to refute the gospel of works and to reemphasize the gospel of salvation by grace through faith.

Word Study: *Adoption of sons*

Huios is the Greek word for *son. Thesis* means *placement.* The compound word *huiothesia* is the word for *adoption.* It corresponds to the Latin *adoptio.* Paul used it in this way in Galatians 4:5 (see also Rom. 8:15; Eph. 1:5). This is one of several words Paul used to describe the tremendous transformation that happens when a sinner believes in Jesus Christ. It connotes the status and "full rights of sons" (NIV).

❖ *Search the Scriptures*

Believers become sons of God through faith in Jesus Christ. This is the most significant reality in a person's life and creates a shared oneness for all believers, regardless of human distinctions. God sent His Son so that those enslaved by sinful powers could be redeemed and become sons of God. He also gives to them the Spirit of His Son.

Made God's Children by Faith (Gal. 3:26-27)

*How do these verses fit into the flow of Paul's argument? Who are the **all** in verse 26? How do the sons of God relate to the Son of God? What kind of **faith** saves? What did Paul mean by **baptized into Christ**? These questions are addressed by comments on these verses.*

3:26-27: **For ye are all the children of God by faith in Christ Jesus.** [27]**For as many of you as have been baptized into Christ have put on Christ.**

In verse 26 Paul introduced a new but related idea into the letter. In 3:6-25, Paul's emphasis was on believers being children of Abraham through faith in Jesus Christ. The Jews claimed that only those who were physical descendants of Abraham were his children

(John 8:33,39; Matt. 3:9). Paul used Genesis 15:6 to show that Abraham was declared righteous based on his faith. When the question arose, "What about the law of Moses?" Paul's answer was that the law was like a slave who disciplined a young child; thus the law led people to see their need for the salvation that came in Jesus Christ.

Whereas 3:6-25 dealt with believers as children of Abraham, verse 26 deals with them as **children of God.** The word is actually *huioi* or "sons" (NIV). Paul wrote of the one unique Son of God (1:15-16; 2:20; 4:4). But those who received Him became children of God (John 1:12). This theme continues through the Focal Passage.

Every word in verse 26 is important. **By faith** shows that the human response to God's grace is **faith.** The opposite of faith is "works" (2:16), which meant obedience to the Jewish law as a means of salvation. Just as Abraham was justified by faith, so are all who are truly saved.

All is another crucial word. In this context, **all** refers to all believers, Jews and Gentiles (see v. 28). Paul's opponents claimed that to receive Israel's Messiah, a person needed to be a Jew—either by birth or by becoming a convert to the Jewish religion (a proselyte). Becoming a proselyte demanded circumcision and obedience to the law. Paul insisted that a Gentile could become a saved person by faith in Christ.

Verse 27 raises the issue of baptism. This is the only mention of baptism in the Letter to the Galatians. Some people make baptism part of the process of salvation. They understand verses like this to mean that water baptism is necessary for salvation and sonship. Timothy George pointed out a major fallacy of this view. Would Paul, who denied that the ritual of circumcision helps to save from sins, have substituted this ritual as necessary for forgiveness? "Was he saying to the Galatians, 'My opponents were wrong in trying to circumcise you. What you really need is to be baptized!'"[1]

The emphasis throughout the letter is on faith as the only way of salvation. What then did Paul mean by verse 27? What is being **baptized into Christ,** and of what importance is it? Paul wrote that it is to **have put on Christ.** The water of baptism signifies this inner experience of coming to Christ—coming to be in Him—and of the new life this leads to. To **put on Christ** seems to refer to removing the old garments of a life of sin and to be clothed in the garments of a new life. Baptism by immersion depicts death, burial, and resurrection—three of these: that of Christ, that of the believer who passes from death to new life, and the future resurrection of the dead.

How do verses 26-27 relate to Christmas? They remind us that the purpose of the coming of the Son of God is not fulfilled in our lives until we through faith come to be sons of God who are in Christ.

Made One in Christ (Gal. 3:28-29)

*What did Paul mean by being **one in Christ Jesus**? Why did he use three examples of human distinctions? What is his main point? What are its implications?*

3:28-29: There is neither Jew nor Greek, there is neither bond nor free, there is neither male nor female: for ye are all one in Christ Jesus. [29]And if ye be Christ's, then are ye Abraham's seed, and heirs according to the promise.

Verses 26-27 set the stage for verse 28. The word **all** in verse 26 led Paul to spell out what this means for human distinctions. He selected three common human distinctions of his day: "Hellenistic men regularly thanked the gods for allowing them to be born as human beings and not beasts, Greeks and not barbarians, citizens and not slaves, men and not women. By the middle of the second century A.D., Rabbi Judah ben Elai had incorporated a similar pattern of 'benedictions' that in slightly revised form can still be found in the Jewish cycle of morning prayers:

Blessed art Thou, O Lord our God, King of the universe, who hast not made me a foreigner.

Blessed art Thou, O Lord our God, King of the universe, who hast not made me a slave.

Blessed art Thou, O Lord our God, King of the universe, who hast not made me a woman."[2]

Paul's main point is debated, but one view is that he was emphasizing that the most important characteristic of every Christian is that the person is **in Christ Jesus.** This reality is more important than belonging to any of the groups by which humans distinguish their group from other groups. In other words, Paul was a Jew, free, and male; but more important, he was **in Christ Jesus.** I am an American Gentile and a white male; but more importantly, I am a Christian.

Being **one in Christ Jesus** has implications about how we treat one another and how we think of ourselves. Paul gave most of his attention to the Jew-Gentile issue. He emphasized that Gentiles could become followers of Christ in the same way as Jews—only through faith.

He also emphasized that when Gentiles became believers they were to be accepted as brothers in Christ.

Verse 28, of course, does not mean that Jews cease to be Jews or Gentiles cease to be Gentiles when they become Christians. Nor in that day did slaves cease to be slaves, although Christian masters were left to struggle with the implications of calling Christian slaves "brothers" (see Philem. 16). Males were still males, and females were still females; however, Paul followed Jesus in helping to raise the status of women from drudges and slaves to human beings. This is consistent with the creation of the male and the female in God's image (Gen. 1:27). Notice that Paul wrote **neither male and female,** not neither husband and wife. He still maintained distinct roles for each, but it was not based on inferior versus superior status.

Verse 29 draws together verses 6-28. After showing that the true children of Abraham are people of faith, Paul showed that they are also children of God through faith in Christ. Those who belong to Christ also belong to the line of Abraham and thus are **heirs according to the promise** made to Abraham and fulfilled in Jesus.

How do these verses relate to our celebration of Christmas? They remind us that the most important thing about any believer is that he or she is **in Christ.** They also emphasize that all who believe are **one in Christ,** regardless of the human categories into which humans divide and identify themselves. Our relation to Christ is more important than any relationship or group.

Redeemed by Christ (Gal. 4:1-5)

*In what sense is an **heir** ever like a slave? What were **the elements of the world**? What is meant by **the fullness of the time**? What is meant by **made of a woman**? What does it mean to be redeemed by Christ? What is involved in being adopted into God's family?*

4:1-3: Now I say, That the heir, as long as he is a child, differeth nothing from a servant, though he be lord of all; [2]but is under tutors and governors until the time appointed of the father. [3]Even so we, when we were children, were in bondage under the elements of the world.

What situation was Paul describing in verses 1-2? He spoke of a time when an **heir** was still a **child.** Paul said that during that time, the **heir** was little more than a **servant** ("slave," NIV, NKJV). In the homes of the first-century rich Roman families, a son often was placed under the care of **tutors** ("guardians," NIV, NKJV, NRSV) **and governors** ("trustees," NIV, NRSV; "stewards," NKJV) while he was still young. These were people who were in some ways like the disciplining slave ("schoolmaster") of 3:24. They had oversight of the child during the years before the child was entrusted with greater responsibility. Even as a child, he and his teachers knew that some day he would be **lord of all** ("owns the whole estate," NIV). This movement from childhood to adulthood happened at **the time appointed of the father.**

Verses 3-5 show that Paul was thinking of the period of redemptive history before Christ came. This was a time of waiting for Jews and Gentiles. Verse 3 also says that it was a time of **bondage.** The Greek word *dedoulomenoi* means "to be enslaved." They were enslaved **under the elements of the world.** The word for **elements** is *stoicheia.* This word has several different uses in the Greek language, and Bible students do not agree on which meaning applies to this verse. There are three possible meanings.

One possible meaning is "elementary things," like the ABCs. This is its meaning in Hebrews 5:12, a plea for believers to move beyond the elementary things of the faith to greater maturity. A second possible meaning focuses on the elements of which the earth is made. In ancient times these were understood to be four: earth, air, fire, and water. This is how the word is used in 2 Peter 3:10,12, which describes the elements of the earth being melted with fervent heat at the end of the world. A third possible meaning relates to the unseen evil spiritual powers, which are opposed to God and His people. This meaning is closely related to a development from the second meaning. The four elements came to be personified in pagan gods and in heavenly bodies, all of which were worshiped by some people. Behind this pagan worship stood the unseen forces of darkness.

Some Bible students believe that verse 3 refers to the elementary kinds of immature religion under which both Jews and Gentiles had been enslaved. Ronald Y. K. Fung wrote, "Certainly what Paul has primarily in view here is the law, and that as an instrument of spiritual bondage."[3] Timothy George suggested that the verse refers to "a whole host of spiritual beings headed by Satan himself."[4] The *New Revised Standard Version* seems to support this view, referring to "the elemental spirits of the world."

We can find support for both of these views elsewhere in the New Testament, even in the writings of Paul. He wrote of being enslaved not only by sin and death but also by the law (Rom. 7:25). And he wrote of the slavery that results from the powers of satanic forces (Eph. 6:10-12). Whatever Paul had in mind in verse 3, he taught that Jesus Christ liberates believers from whatever enslaves them.

4:4-5: But when the fullness of the time was come, God sent forth his Son, made of a woman, made under the law, [5]to redeem them that were under the law, that we might receive the adoption of sons.

These are the most familiar verses in the passage and are often used at Christmas. They tell of the *when, who,* and *why* of God's plan. In **the fullness of the time** refers to what is called in verse 2 **the time appointed of the father.** God chose the time to send His Son into the world. Many have noted the various ways in which God had prepared the world for this time. Jesus came into a world when one language—Greek—was known to almost everyone. This facilitated the spreading of the gospel. Another factor that aided the early missionaries was the dispersion of the Jews. This meant that there were synagogues in most cities. The Roman Empire had brought good roads, no national borders, and an era of peace. But God did not choose this time because conditions were right; He worked in the affairs of nations to make the conditions fit His time.

God sent forth his Son is the good news in a nutshell. It shows that Jesus' coming was no accident of history. It also shows that Jesus was the divine Son before He came. He was not chosen from among humans to be the Son of God. He was the divine Son or Word from eternity. But at the right time, God sent His Son into the world.

Made ("born," NIV, NKJV) **of a woman** may have one or more of the following meanings. A choice is hard since all three possibilities are taught elsewhere in the Bible. One view is that passages like Job 14:1 are in the background. The Hebrews used "born of woman" as synonymous with being human. According to this view, Paul had just stressed the deity of the Son; now he emphasized that the Son was fully human as well as fully divine (see also John 1:1-2,14). Another view is that the words reflect a fulfillment of the promise in Genesis 3:15 that the seed of the woman would crush the tempter. A third view is that the words may at least imply the virgin birth of Jesus, so clearly taught in Matthew 1 and Luke 1–2. In a sermon on this text, Herschel H. Hobbs said, "Paul does not mention specifically the virgin birth of Jesus. But in this statement he strongly implies it."[5]

Made ("born," NIV, NKJV) **under the law** refers to the birth of Jesus as a Jew, thus to the people to whom God had given the law. Jesus had no patience with the many human traditions the Pharisees had burdened the people with, but He fulfilled and interpreted the law as God intended. He met all its demands.

He was **made under the law** in order **to redeem them that were under the law. Redeem** is the same word found in 3:13, *exagorase*. The emphasis in on purchasing something, and it was used to refer to setting a slave free by paying the redemption price.

Paul referred to the death of Christ as the means of redeeming sinners from the curse of the law (3:13). This cost of redemption is implicit here in verse 5. Sinners are slaves of forces from which they cannot deliver themselves, but the death and resurrection of Christ sets us free.

The positive purpose of God's sending His Son was **that we might receive the adoption of sons. Adoption** seems to imply the receiving of orphans into full sonship, but Paul's use in verses 1-5 seems to stress moving from the slave-like condition of immature heirs to be made full heirs and sons. Either way we apply it today, the emphasis is on God's love in making us full sons and heirs of Him as our Heavenly Father.

At this Christmas season, we do well to take seriously the true purposes for which God sent His Son: to set us free from the slavery of sin, death, and Satan; and to make us His children. True children of God love Him and one another.

Given the Spirit of Christ (Gal. 4:6-7)

What is the relation between adoption and receiving the Spirit? What names are used for the Holy Spirit? How is the Trinity depicted in these verses?

4:6-7: And because ye are sons, God hath sent forth the Spirit of his Son into your hearts, crying, Abba, Father. [7]Wherefore thou art no more a servant, but a son; and if a son, then an heir of God through Christ.

One of the realities that accompanies becoming a child of God is receiving the **Spirit.** It is hard to say which comes first because they are so closely related. Here Paul wrote that **because ye are sons, God hath sent forth the Spirit of his Son into your hearts.** The experience of adoption and the reception of the Spirit are inseparable.

The Holy Spirit is described by a number of titles in the New Testament. He is the Holy Spirit, the Spirit, the Spirit of God, the Spirit of Christ, and **the Spirit of his Son.** All of these titles refer to the same unseen presence of God. The emphasis in the title in verse 6 is on the continuing work of the Son of God through His Spirit. God the Father sent both into the world. God sent His Son to redeem sinners and to adopt them as His children. He sent the Spirit of His Son to continue the work begun in the life, death, and resurrection of Jesus.

Sent forth is the same Greek word used in verse 4 for God's sending forth His Son. We are Trinitarian Christians for two reasons. This is the way the one God has revealed Himself, and this is the way we have experienced Him. He is the Father above us to whom we pray and whom we worship. He is the Son who became flesh to reveal the Father and to save us from our sins. He is the Spirit who moves in our **hearts** and among our fellowship.

It is through the Spirit that believers cry, **Abba, Father.** He is the One who helps us pray when words fail us (Rom. 8:26). Here is the paradox of God within us helping us pray to God above us.

Verse 7 is another summary verse. It ties together Galatians 3:6–4:7. Each believer in Christ is **no more a servant, but a son; and if a son, then an heir of God through Christ.** We are freed from our earlier slavery and are now children of God, full heirs of the promise to Abraham.

Traditionally at Christmas we think of Jesus in the manger and all that led up to that and what immediately followed. However, we need to remember that the manger now is empty. The One who came into the world as a babe in a manger went on to a ministry that ended in His death for our sins. However, we need to remember that now the cross is empty because Jesus finished the work of atoning for our sins. He was placed in a tomb, but now the tomb is empty because He was raised from the dead. We might visit the land where He lived during the days of His ministry, but He is not there in the flesh. Where then is He? Paul reminded us that God sent the Spirit of His Son into our hearts.

> Thou didst leave Thy throne and Thy kingly crown,
> When Thou camest to earth for me;
> But in Bethlehem's home was there found no room
> For Thy holy nativity.
> O, come to my heart, Lord Jesus,
> There is room in my heart for Thee.

Thou camest, O Lord, with the living word
That should set Thy people free;
But with mocking scorn, and with crown of thorn,
They bore Thee to Calvary.
O, come to my heart, Lord Jesus,
There is room in my heart for Thee.[6]

❖ *Spiritual Transformations*

Paul stressed that believers in Christ are children of God through faith. This reality of being in Christ is the most important thing about any believer—transcending such human distinctions as race, economic status, or gender. Before Christ came, people were enslaved by forces from which they could not set themselves free; however, when God sent His Son to redeem sinners and to adopt them as His children, God also sent the Spirit of His Son into our hearts as assurance of our relationship as children and heirs of God.

Throughout the comments on these verses we have asked how each block of verses relates to Christmas. We have noted four related applications: (1) The purpose of the coming of the Son of God is not fulfilled in our lives until we through faith come to be sons of God who are in Christ. (2) Our relationship to Christ is more important than any relationship or group. (3) God sent His Son to set us free from the slavery of sin, death, and Satan, and to make us His children. (4) God sent the Spirit of His Son into our hearts.

When were you redeemed from sin and adopted as a child of God?

_____

What do you need to do now to prepare for a Christian Christmas?

_____

Prayer of Commitment: Lord, help me keep Christmas as a redeemed child of Yours.

[1]Timothy George, "Galatians," in *The New American Commentary*, vol. 30 [Nashville: Broadman & Holman Publishers, 1994], 277.

[2]Quoted in George, "Galatians," NAC, 285.

[3]Ronald Y. K. Fung, *The Epistle to the Galatians*, in The New International Commentary on the New Testament [Grand Rapids: William B. Eerdmans Publishing Company, 1988], 181.

[4]George, "Galatians," NAC, 298.

[5]Herschel H. Hobbs, "God's Answer to Man's Predicament," *The Beam*, October 1966, 53.

[6]Emily E. S. Elliott, "Thou Didst Leave Thy Throne," *The Baptist Hymnal* [Nashville: Convention Press, 1991], No. 121.

THE HOPE OF CHRISTMAS

Bible Passage: Romans 15:1-13
Key Verse: Romans 15:12

❖ *Significance of the Lesson*

• The *Theme* of this lesson is that by sending Jesus through the line of Jesse, God fulfilled a promise that gives hope to all people.
• The *Life Question* this lesson seeks to address is, How does Christmas give me hope?
• The *Biblical Truth* is that God's fulfilling His promise to send the Messiah through Jesse's line evidences His faithfulness to keep His word, which gives people hope.
• The *Life Impact* is to help you have the hope that God gives.

False and True Hopes

People with a secular worldview cling to hopes in the sense of wishful thinking or of wistful longing for dreams to come true. Their hopes are based on their own intellects and abilities, good luck, and others' help or provision. Thus many secular people have no real basis for true hope. When their hopes fail, they often fall into despair.

The biblical worldview affirms that God is true to His word; He keeps His promises. People can trust Him and His intentions for them. This gives them confident hope, which is based on what God can do, not on what humans can do.

Hope—One of *God's Big Little Words*

My doctoral dissertation in seminary was on the meaning of the Greek word for "hope" (*elpis*). This short everyday word was filled with new significance in the New Testament. Later I wrote *God's Big Little Words*.[1] The thesis of the book is that the "big" words in the Bible in terms of use and importance are the "little" or short words. Five words were used to demonstrate this: life, love, hope, joy, and peace. These words are short in Greek and in English. Yet if you look each up in a concordance, you will find many uses of each one. They—more than the long words—carry the real message of the Bible. And these words also express what people today are seeking. People are searching for life, love, hope, joy, and peace.

This lesson focuses on hope, but the Bible Passage mentions also joy and peace. All five of these words are found in the gospel story, especially in the account of the birth of Jesus. These are key words for the Christmas season. The tragedy is that many people find only bogus forms of each of these. The true forms of each can only be found in God.

Word Study: *Confirm*

The Greek word translated "confirm" in Romans 15:8 is *bebaiosai*. The word means to "make firm," "establish," or "confirm." It is used of persons and things. First Corinthians 1:6,8 gives examples of each. Verse 6 relates to confirming the testimony of Christ, and verse 8 relates to confirming and strengthening believers.

❖ *Search the Scriptures*

Paul called on the mature believers to help build up their weaker brothers. He prayed that all believers would glorify God with one spirit and one voice. Recalling promises of God's plan to include Gentiles, Paul called on Jewish and Gentile believers to praise God as they found the God of hope filled them with joy and peace.

Build Up Others (Rom. 15:1-4)

*Who were the **strong**? Who were the **weak**? With which group did Paul identify himself? What debt did the one group owe the other? How did Paul use the word **please**? How should believers build up one another? How did Paul use Jesus as an example? How can the Old Testament be of help to Christians? What is the basic meaning of the word **hope**? How do the Scriptures provide hope?* These questions are addressed in comments on these verses.

Verse 1: **We then that are strong ought to bear the infirmities of the weak, and not to please ourselves.**

Paul used the word *dunatoi* in verse 1 to describe a group he called the **strong.** He used the negative of this word (*adunaton*) to describe the **weak.** Paul's use of **we** shows that he considered himself one of the strong. Who were these groups? The word **infirmities** can be translated "scruples" (NKJV). The weakness of this group, from Paul's point of view, was that they had strict scruples about issues that restricted them and the church in exercising their freedom in Christ. Apparently these scruples represented both Jewish and Gentile views. Thus not all the strong were Gentiles, and not all the weak were Jews.

The word **ought** expresses an obligation. It was used for monetary debts and for moral obligations. The strong were **to bear the infirmities of the weak. Bear** is the same word Paul used in Galatians 6:2 in a call to bear one another's burdens. It is more than a passive putting up with others. His following words show that Paul was calling for self-giving love. This is what he meant when he wrote **not to please ourselves.**

Verses 2-3: **Let everyone of us please his neighbor for his good to edification. [3]For even Christ pleased not himself; but, as it is written, The reproaches of them that reproached thee fell on me.**

Paul explained what he meant in the last part of verse 1. He used the word **please** to describe what people do when they put their own interests first. Instead of pleasing ourselves, we are to **please** our **neighbor for his good.** Both the word **neighbor** and the word **good** make clear that Paul was thinking of the kind of Christian love that does **good** for others. The use of **neighbor** reminds us of the command, "Love thy neighbor as thyself" (13:9). There is a sinful kind of pleasing others that compromises one's faith to win the approval of others (Gal. 1:10). Paul was not talking about that. This is clear because Jesus Christ is our model for what Paul meant: **Christ pleased not himself.** For proof of this Paul quoted Psalm 69:9: **The reproaches of them that reproached thee fell on me.**

Verse 4: **For whatsoever things were written aforetime were written for our learning, that we through patience and comfort of the scriptures might have hope.**

After quoting from the Old Testament, Paul wrote about the value of **the scriptures**—the Old Testament—for Christians. They **were written aforetime** ("in the past," NIV; "in former days," NRSV). They **were written for our learning** ("instruction," NRSV). The purpose was **that we through patience** ("endurance, NIV) **and comfort** ("encouragement," NIV) **of the scriptures might have hope. Patience** means "to bear up under pressure." **Comfort** can mean "exhortation" or "encouragement."

The *King James Version* and the *New International Version* reflect two slightly different ways of translating this verse. The *King James Version* understands these two words to be characteristics of the Scriptures. The *New International Version*'s rendering, "through endurance and the encouragement of the Scriptures we might have hope," emphasizes encouragement as a characteristic of the Scriptures.

The inspired Scriptures are God's Word. God speaks to each of us and to each generation through the Bible. Paul drew lessons from Old Testament personalities in passages such as Romans 4 and 1 Corinthians 10:1-11. The writer of Hebrews pointed to examples of faith in the Old Testament (Heb. 11).

In Sunday School we look into the Bible each week for lessons for life. We do this throughout our lives because God's Word continues to instruct us throughout each age of life. If you are using these materials in the Family Bible Series for a Family Bible Time, you know that the same passage can speak a relevant message to different age groups. No one ever graduates in this life from Bible study.

Paul here reminded us that one of the strong messages of the Bible is **hope. Hope** can be looked at from three perspectives: the experience of hope, the basis for hope, and the goal of hope. As used by the Greeks, the word combined desire with expectation. The Christian experience adds a third element—confidence. This confidence is based on the fact that Christian hope has its foundation in the God of hope. Those without Christ have no real hope (Eph. 2:12; 1 Thess. 4:13). They may have many hopes of their own, but they lack the solid hope that comes through the Lord—a hope about which we learn in the Word of God.

Glorify God (Rom. 15:5-6)

*What titles describe God? What did Paul mean by **likeminded**? Why are verses 5-6 considered a prayer? How does being likeminded **glorify God**?*

Verses 5-6: Now the God of patience and consolation grant you to be likeminded one toward another according to Christ Jesus:

⁶that ye may with one mind and one mouth glorify God, even the Father of our Lord Jesus Christ.

Verses 5-6 contain two titles for God. Using the same two Greek words from verse 4 about the Scriptures, Paul called Him **the God of patience and consolation.** The reason that the Scriptures have these two qualities is that they are the Word of God, and God is the One who helps people endure and who encourages them with hope. He is also called **God, even the Father of our Lord Jesus Christ.** This title emphasizes that the only true God is the God whose unique Son Jesus Christ was sent into the world to reveal God and to save sinners.

Robert H. Mounce commented on **likeminded:** "His desire that they 'mind the same thing among one another' (literal translation) does not mean that they should all come to the same conclusion. That is obvious from his discussion of the weak and the strong—the conscience of each is to guide the conduct of that person. It is unity of perspective that is desired. And that perspective is that of Jesus Christ, our model for Christian conduct."[2]

According to Christ Jesus can be translated "as you follow Christ Jesus" (NIV). **With one mind and one mouth** ("with one accord you may with one voice," NASB) does not demand uniformity, but it does call for a spirit of oneness of spirit and purpose. Such unity of spirit will **glorify God.** To **glorify God** is to praise Him so that His reputation is equal to His character. Jesus said that the world would recognize His disciples by their love for one another (John 13:35). We don't have to agree about peripheral things to treat fellow believers as brothers and sisters and to worship the Lord together. Christians in a church need to learn how to disagree without becoming disagreeable. A church fight does not glorify God. To the contrary, it brings reproach on God and His church.

One of the great things about Christmas is its potential for bringing people together—families, churches, and believers of different denominations. Even non-Christians often know familiar Christmas carols and the Christmas story. Believers can build on these to tell the true meaning of Christ's coming.

The word **grant** ("give," NIV) shows that verses 5-6 are a prayer. Paul prayed to God for the kind of oneness of spirit that would glorify God. This kind of unity in a church, a family, or another group is the gift of God. Only He can make it a reality. May God grant that your family and mine, your church and mine, may have this type of togetherness at this Christmas season and into the future.

Radiate Hope (Rom. 15:7-13)

*How and why should Christians **receive one another**? How does Christ offer hope to Jews and to Gentiles? Why did Paul quote so many similar Old Testament verses? What is distinctive about Christian hope?*

Verse 7: Wherefore receive ye one another, as Christ also received us to the glory of God.

The word **receive** can also be translated "accept" (NIV) or "welcome" (NRSV). It is the opposite of rejecting or refusing. Paul used the same word in 14:1 to exhort the strong to receive the weak in the faith. In 14:3, he said to receive them because God had received them. In 15:7 Paul wrote that believers should **receive . . . one another, as Christ also received us.** (Some ancient manuscripts of Romans read "you," as in the NIV and HCSB.)

How does Christ receive people? During His ministry He was criticized for receiving sinners and for even eating with them (Luke 15:1-2). Jesus then told three parables to show that God welcomes repentant sinners. This is epitomized in the father's warm welcome for the prodigal son (vv. 24,32). Jesus welcomes all kinds of people, no matter who they are or how great their sins.

Paul's point is that just as Jesus received us in spite of our sins, so should we welcome others whom He has welcomed. If Christ has received someone, who are we to reject the person? When we follow the example of Jesus in this, we do so **to the glory of God.**

Over a century ago, F. L. Godet wrote words that still apply: "The compassionate welcome which Christ has given to all the members of the church individually ought to be perpetually reproduced in the welcome of goodwill and tenderness which they give one another in all the relations of life."[3]

Verses 8-12: Now I say that Jesus Christ was a minister of the circumcision for the truth of God, to confirm the promises made unto the fathers: [9]and that the Gentiles might glorify God for his mercy; as it is written, For this cause I will confess to thee among the Gentiles, and sing unto thy name. [10]And again he saith, Rejoice, ye Gentiles, with his people. [11]And again, Praise the Lord, all ye Gentiles; and laud him, all ye people. [12]And again, Isaiah saith, There shall be a root of Jesse, and he that shall rise to reign over the Gentiles; in him shall the Gentiles trust.

These verses show that in verses 1-13 Paul was speaking of the need of Jewish believers and Gentile believers to receive one another. Jesus came to fulfill God's promises to the Jewish people and to carry out His intention to offer salvation also to Gentiles. The first of these is seen in the last part of verse 8 and the other in the first part of verse 9. Paul had a double purpose. He wanted to remind Gentile believers that it was through the Jews that they had the opportunity to be included among God's people. He wanted Jews to realize that God's purpose always has been to extend His love to Gentiles.

Jesus Christ was a minister of the circumcision refers to His mission to the Jews. **For the truth of God** reminds us that one of the meanings of **truth** is "faithfulness" or "dependability." God always has been true to His word. He made **promises** to **the fathers.** He kept those promises to people of faith in Old Testament times. Among these promises were not only those to the Jews but also some concerning Gentiles. Paul wanted the Gentile believers to recognize that God's promises to the Jews included them. Paul's purpose in reminding Gentiles of this was **that the Gentiles might glorify God for his mercy.**

This truth was supported by four quotations from the Scriptures. Each of these shows God's purpose for Gentiles as well as Jews. This is not surprising since Paul was a missionary to the Gentiles. His life was given to take the good news to them and to promote fellowship of Jewish and Gentile believers. One of the high points of the 2000 Summer Olympics in Sydney, Australia, was the closing ceremony. In the opening ceremony each nation's athletes marched in with the athletes from their own country. In the closing ceremony athletes from all the nations were mingled together. If a common interest in athletics can bring together different people, how much more should the good news of Jesus Christ!

As it is written introduces the first of four Old Testament quotations in verse 9. It is from 2 Samuel 22:50, which also is found in Psalm 18:49. David was thanking God for giving him victory over his enemies. Commenting on Paul's use of this verse, Douglas J. Moo wrote: "Paul may cite the verse as a claim of the risen Christ. And this possibility gains credence when we note the context of the verse that Paul quotes. For David's praise of God 'among the Gentiles' is stimulated by the fact that God has given him victory over Gentile nations. God has made him 'the head of the nations,' so that a 'people whom I had not known served me' (v. 43). It would fit Paul's purposes perfectly if he were attributing to Christ this praise of God for the subduing of the Gentiles under his messianic rule."[4]

Therefore, I will praise you among the Gentiles;

I will sing hymns to your name (v. 9, NIV).

Paul's second quotation is from Deuteronomy 32:43. Moses called on the nations to rejoice over the salvation of Israel. Paul saw it as a call for **Gentiles** to **rejoice . . . with his people.**

In verse 11 Paul quoted Psalm 117:1. **Praise the Lord, all ye Gentiles; and laud him, all ye people.** In verse 12 Paul quoted Isaiah 11:10. The **root of Jesse** was a messianic title. Thus the Messiah **shall rise to reign over the Gentiles; in him shall the Gentiles trust.** The word **trust** is actually the verb for "hope" (NIV, HCSB, NKJV). This is an example of the biblical basis for hope. This hope is on a solid foundation because it is hope in God, not hope in ourselves, in others, or in luck.

***Verse 13:* Now the God of hope fill you with all joy and peace in believing, that ye may abound in hope, through the power of the Holy Ghost.**

The biblical foundation for hope can be expressed as hope in God or as **the God of hope.** This means that God is the One who gives hope and the One on whom we build our hope. **Hope** is closely related to **joy and peace.** Paul prayed that **the God of hope fill you with all joy and peace. Joy** and **peace** occur in the Christmas story (Luke 2:10,14). Romans 12:12 has "rejoicing in hope" as one Christian characteristic. Romans 14:17 says, "The kingdom of God is not meat and drink; but righteousness, and peace, and joy in the Holy Ghost."

Verse 13 is a prayer. Only God can give **hope . . . joy . . . peace.** The word **believing** shows that these qualities come from God to believers. They are not qualities that nonbelievers can develop on their own. Secular people often assume that changing outward circumstances can create these experiences. Such people may have hopes, joys, and times of peace; but only God can give the real thing.

Verse 13 begins and ends with hope. **The God of hope** fills believers with joy and peace in order that believers **may abound in hope, through the power of the Holy Ghost. Joy and peace** are listed among the fruit of the Spirit (Gal. 5:22). **Hope** is also something that is made possible by the Spirit.

Christmas is a time of hope, joy, and peace. Yet at times when many are celebrating, others are sunk into deep despair. Life has fallen in on them, and they feel it most when others seem to be rejoicing. God through His Spirit and through the ministry of Christian friends can often help despairing people have renewed hope, joy, and peace.

As Phillips Brooks put it so long ago:

The hopes and fears of all the years
Are met in thee tonight.[5]

❖ *Spiritual Transformations*

Paul closed the body of the Book of Romans by calling on the strong to bear the burdens of the weak and thus to build them up. He prayed for the kind of unity of spirit that glorifies God. After calling on all believers to welcome one another, he quoted Old Testament passages relating to Jews and Gentiles. He prayed that the God of hope would fill believers with joy and peace in believing.

Do you have the hope that only God gives? The experience of this kind of hope is more than wishful thinking; it adds confidence to desire and expectation. The basis for this confident hope is the God of hope, who gives it and on whom it is based. The goal for this hope is the fulfillment of God's purposes for His people.

To determine whether you have this kind of hope, ask yourself these questions:

To what degree is my hope confident hope, not wishful thinking?

_____

To what degree is my hope based on what only God can do? ____

_____

To what degree is my hope focused on God's purpose for His people?

_____

Prayer of Commitment: Great God of hope, fill me with the kind of hope that only You can give.

[1]Robert J. Dean, *God's Big Little Words*. Nashville: Broadman Press, 1975.

[2]Robert H. Mounce, "Romans," in *The New American Commentary*, vol. 27 [Nashville: Broadman & Holman Publishers, 1995], 260.

[3]F. L. Godet, *Commentary on the Epistle to the Romans* [Grand Rapids: Zondervan Publishing Company, 1883, reprint], 470.

[4]Douglas J. Moo, *The Epistle to the Romans*, in The New International Commentary on the New Testament [Grand Rapids: William B. Eerdmans Publishing Company, 1996], 878-879.

[5]Phillips Brooks, "O Little Town of Bethlehem," No. 86, *The Baptist Hymnal*, 1991.

Week of December 16

THE PERSON OF CHRISTMAS

Background Passage: Luke 2:1-20
Focal Passage: Luke 2:4-20
Key Verses: Luke 2:10-11

❖ *Significance of the Lesson*

• The *Theme* of this lesson is Christmas is the celebration of Jesus' birth.
• The *Life Question* this lesson seeks to address is, How will I celebrate Jesus' birth?
• The *Biblical Truth* is that Jesus' birth was a joyous occasion that calls for continuing celebration.
• The *Life Impact* is to help you consistently keep Jesus' birth at the center of your celebration of Christmas.

Christmas or Holiday Season?

In the secular worldview the birth of Jesus does not matter. If it actually occurred, it was nothing more than the birth of another figure of history. Secular people value Christmas only as a holiday season with time off from work. Some use it primarily as a commercial time of buying and selling. Some use it as an excuse for indulgence.

In the biblical worldview the birth of Jesus has eternal implications. Jesus' birth signaled God's acting to redeem His people from their sins. Just as the angels called the shepherds to rejoice in the coming of the Savior, Christ the Lord, so do believers continue to celebrate His birth.

Luke 2:1-20: A Familiar Passage

This is one of the most familiar Bible passages. We often study it at Christmas. Adults who attend Sunday School, therefore, are very familiar with it. There is a danger in studying such passages that people will assume that they already have learned everything possible about such a passage. A teacher is faced with the challenge of leading learners to look at and feel its impact anew. Therefore, the commentary on this lesson will use a slightly different approach. The format will be questions to various people involved in Luke 2:1-20: Luke, Joseph, Mary, a shepherd, and an angel of the Lord.

If you are a teacher, you can use this material in several ways: (1) You can ignore the format and use the material in making your own lecture. (2) You can ask the questions for the entire class to discuss. (3) You can have some members role-play each person. Give each group or team time to decide how they think the person would have answered the questions. Then interview them and ask each to respond as if the member were that person.

(Note: Of course, none of these persons were actually interviewed. The answers in the commentary are my idea of how they might have answered. I have followed views held by evangelical Bible students. Where additional comments are needed, these follow the answers.)

Word Study: *Joy*

"Joy" in Luke 2:10 translates *charan*. The angel announced "good tidings of great joy, which shall be for all people." *Joy* in the Bible differs from what most people mean by happiness and pleasure. Happiness and pleasure are human emotions that people seek to create by changing outward circumstances. Christian joy is the result of a right relation with God, and it continues even in times of trouble. The word does have a celebrative aspect to it in passages like this one.

❖ *Search the Scriptures*

The birth of Jesus in humble circumstances was a momentous event in the history of humanity and God's redemptive purpose. The glorious good news announced to the shepherds by the angel and the heavenly host calls on believers to continue to celebrate the coming of the Savior. The joyful response of the shepherds to their visit to see Jesus is an example of the joy that should characterize our celebrations of His birth.

The Momentous Event (Luke 2:4-7)

Verses 4-7: **And Joseph also went up from Galilee, out of the city of Nazareth, into Judea, unto the city of David, which is called**

Bethlehem; (because he was of the house and lineage of David:) [5]to be taxed with Mary his espoused wife, being great with child. [6]And so it was, that, while they were there, the days were accomplished that she should be delivered. [7]And she brought forth her firstborn son, and wrapped him in swaddling clothes, and laid him in a manger; because there was no room for them in the inn.

Luke, why did you write your Gospel? "As I wrote in my prologue (1:1-4), I wanted to write an orderly account of the good news of Jesus, which was based on the testimony of eyewitnesses, and which would show the certainty of the events about which we had been taught."

The apostles were the eyewitnesses of the life of Jesus. They were getting older and some of them had died. Others were beginning to write what the apostles had taught. Luke wrote in 1:1-4 that he felt led to write an orderly account of the things Christians believed. This is one reason for his inclusion of historical references such as 1:5; 2:1-2; 3:1. These references grounded the Bible events in history.

Luke, why did you spend so much time on events surrounding the birth of Jesus? "I felt that the coming of Christ was the most momentous event of redemptive history to date. The climax of His ministry in His death and resurrection was crucial, but those events were foreshadowed by His birth."

Luke 1:5–2:39 tells of the events related to Jesus' birth and infancy. Matthew 1:18–2:23 tells of other events and of some of the same events from the perspective of Joseph. These two writers under the leadership of the Spirit included many details about Jesus' conception and birth. They obviously believed that these events were momentous in God's redemptive plan.

Joseph, why did you make the long journey from Nazareth to Bethlehem? "Caesar Augustus issued a decree that all people in the Roman Empire register for taxation. We Jews were told to go to our tribal ancestral city, which in my case was Bethlehem."

Nazareth was about 90 miles from **Bethlehem,** and much of this journey was uphill. Thus Joseph **went up** in this long trip. It was a several-day journey. This was not a census that was taken at home but by ancestral tribes. Thus Joseph, being from the tribe of Judah, had to go to **Bethlehem,** which was called **the city of David** because it was the place of David's birth. Micah 5:2 prophesied that the Messiah, or future Davidic King, would be born in Bethlehem. God used the decree of the Roman emperor in faraway Rome to set in motion a process that brought Mary and Joseph to Bethlehem at just the right time for the birth of Jesus.

Joseph, were you and Mary married or only betrothed when you took this trip? "We had been betrothed, but after the angel spoke to me about the unique manner of her conception, we were married. However, we had not come together as husband and wife and would not until after the birth of this special child."

Espoused wife translates *emnesteumene*. Strictly speaking, the word refers to the betrothal or engagement. According to Matthew 1:20, however, the angel of the Lord told Joseph not to be afraid to take Mary as his wife. Verses 24-25 states that they were married but that they did not have sexual relations until after the birth of Jesus. Luke may have used the word for betrothal because, although married, Joseph and Mary had not consummated their marriage.

Joseph, why did you take Mary on this long trip? "Mary is my wife. God had entrusted her care to me. She was soon to bear a special son. Although the journey was long and hard, we did not want to be separated at such a time."

Some Bible students believe that Mary went because she also had to register for taxation. Many translations (as the KJV) imply that the words **with Mary** go with **to be taxed.** Others link the words with **went up.** "Luke's point is not that they registered together, but that they traveled together."[1]

Mary, how did you become pregnant? "The angel Gabriel appeared to me and told me that I was to bear a special child, who would be the Son of God. When I asked how this was possible since I was a virgin, Gabriel told me that the child would be conceived by the Holy Spirit."

The biblical account of this is in Luke 1:26-35. Joseph found out about it as described in Matthew 1:18-23. This was obviously a miracle. The people of the first century knew that a virgin did not bear a child. As a physician, Luke surely knew this; yet he believed in the virgin birth of Jesus.

Mary, were you mistreated by the people of Bethlehem? "Not really. It is true that we could find no good accommodations better than a place where animals were kept, but many homes of the time had animals in part of the house. We were glad to be allowed to find shelter in the humble place where Jesus was born."

Bible students debate the meaning of the last part of verse 7. Some assume that the mention of **no room for them in the inn** implies a callous innkeeper who refused them a place to stay. Others note that the text does not say anything about an innkeeper. Robert H. Stein pointed out: "This does not refer to the lack of a 'hotel room' but lack of a suitable 'place' for Mary to give birth to her son. It does not imply any rejection on the part of the much maligned innkeeper. The 'inn' probably refers to a public caravansary (a crude overnight lodging place for caravans), which was the one lodging place in Bethlehem."[2] Bible students debate exactly where they were. But it was some place where animals were kept, for a **manger** was a feeding trough for an animal.

Mary, if the birth of Jesus was so momentous, why was He born in such humble circumstances? "God could have chosen a princess to bear His Son and have Him born in a palace, but He chose me, a humble girl, to bear Him; and He led us to the place in Bethlehem."

This humble beginning is consistent with the Servant role of Jesus (see Mark 10:45; Phil. 2:5-8).

This momentous event literally split history in two. Oscar Cullmann in his book *Christ and Time* pointed out that Jesus came at the midpoint of redemptive history. We date our years from the time of His birth (A.D. is from the Latin *anno Domini*, "the year of the Lord"), and we date the years before His birth (B.C. is "Before Christ"). Earlier systems dated ahead from a fixed point. The Jewish calendar, for example, is dated from the supposed date of the creation. The Roman calendar was dated from the traditional date for the founding of Rome. The Bible and other ancient literature often dated events from the beginning of the reign of a king or ruler (see 3:1).

Cullmann noted that the unique thing about the Christian system is that it sees the coming of Jesus as the key to all that preceded and all that followed. He wrote: "Our system, however, does not proceed from an initial point, but from *a center*; it takes as the mid-point an event which is open to historical investigation and can be chronologically fixed, if not with complete accuracy, at least within a space of a few years. This event is the birth of Jesus Christ of Nazareth. Thence proceed in opposite directions two enumerations, one forward, the other backward: 'after Christ,' 'before Christ.'"[3]

The Glorious Good News (Luke 2:8-14)

Verses 8-14: And there were in the same country shepherds abiding in the field, keeping watch over their flock by night. [9]And,

lo, the angel of the Lord came upon them, and the glory of the Lord shone round about them: and they were sore afraid. [10]And the angel said unto them, Fear not: for, behold, I bring you good tidings of great joy, which shall be to all people. [11]For unto you is born this day in the city of David a Savior, which is Christ the Lord. [12]And this shall be a sign unto you; Ye shall find the babe wrapped in swaddling clothes, lying in a manger. [13]And suddenly there was with the angel a multitude of the heavenly host praising God, and saying, [14]Glory to God in the highest, and on earth peace, good will toward men.

Shepherd, what were you doing when the angel appeared to you? "We were watching over our sheep during the night. Sheep need lots of care and protection, so one or more of us was always on watch."

We are not told whether the sheep were in a fold of some kind or were simply gathered together. Either way, shepherds had to protect them from thieves and wild animals.

Shepherd, what time of the year was this? "I'm not good at keeping up with dates, but the weather was warm enough for us to be outside with the sheep."

Herschel H. Hobbs wrote: "Of course, the traditional time is December 25. However, the fact that the sheep were in the fields suggests a time between March and November, the time when they were kept out in the open."[4] Actually the New Testament does not tell us the date of Jesus' birth, nor does it call for an annual celebration of it. This custom developed in the centuries after the first century. Several dates were tried, but finally December 25 was chosen. Some Christian groups have objected to such a celebration, but most have embraced it as an opportunity to celebrate the birth of Jesus.

Shepherd, do you believe in angels? "I believe in angels because one appeared to us and then an entire host of angels spoke, praising God. The first awareness we had of this was the radiant brightness that suddenly flooded the place. Then an angel spoke to us. At first we were terrified, but the angel told us not to be frightened."

The angel of the Lord came upon them ("stood before them," NKJV, HCSB; "appeared to them," NIV). **Glory** is *doxa*, the brightness and splendor of the Lord. This **shone round about them. Sore afraid** is a combination of the Greek verb and noun for fear—*ephobethesan phobon*—together with the word "great" (*megan*), which literally means "to fear with a great fear." Angels are prominent throughout the biblical account of the events surrounding the birth of Jesus. An angel also appeared to Zechariah, to Mary, and to Joseph.

Angel, why did you make the first announcement of the birth of Jesus to shepherds? "God made the choice; we angels are only messengers. Shepherds are among the lower class of people. God was trying to show that His Son came not for the high and mighty but for the poor and lowly."

Some Bible students also feel that respectable people considered shepherds dishonest sinners. This too might be part of the answer. In any case, they were not the first group that most people would expect to hear the good news of the birth of Jesus. In this respect, the shepherds are like the wise men. The wise men represented not poor Jews but pagan Gentiles. The New Testament shows that Jesus came for rich and poor, Jews and Gentiles.

Angel, what was the good news that you announced? "I was sent by God to tell them of the birth of the Savior, who was the Messiah and the Lord. This good news was a message of joy for all people."

Verses 10-12 is the angel's message. **Bring . . . good tidings** translates one of Luke's favorite words *euangelizomai*, from which we get our word *evangelize*. It means "to proclaim good news." This word is found 11 times in the Gospels, 10 of which are in Luke. In the New Testament it usually refers, as it does here, to the good news about Jesus Christ. The good news brought **great joy** to replace the great fear. This is especially important in a lesson that focuses on celebration, for joy is at the heart of any Christian celebration.

Verse 11 focuses on three titles for Jesus. **Savior** (*soter*) was used to describe deliverers from various kinds of dangers. The word often was used of Roman emperors. However, Jesus came to save from sin (Matt. 1:21). **Christ** (*christos*) is the Greek version of the Hebrew *messiah*. Both words mean "the anointed one." Kings in ancient times were anointed with oil. In biblical use the term referred to the coming King of David's line who would establish an eternal kingdom. **Lord** (*kurios*) refers to the deity of the newborn child. The combination of these three terms is powerful testimony to the uniqueness of the One whose birth the angel declared to be **good tidings of great joy, which shall be to all people.**

One of the strong themes of the two books written by Luke is that the good news was intended for **all people.** This is implicit in the Gospel and explicit in the Book of Acts.

Angel, how did the words of the heavenly host supplement the good news you announced? "The heavenly host were a host of special angels who praised God for the announcement of the good news. Their praise focused on glory that is due to God in heaven and peace that comes by His grace to people on earth."

The word for **praising** (*ainounton*) is used in the Bible only of praises to God. This is one way of celebrating the birth of Jesus—whether the praises are in songs, prayers, or testimonies. The praises included what takes place in heaven **(in the highest)** and what takes place **on earth.** The focus in heaven is on **glory to God.** The focus on earth is on **peace, good will toward men.** The words **good will toward men** translate *anthropois eudokia.* Other old manuscripts have *anthropois eudokias.* Although only one letter is different, the second version changes the case of the noun. The second reading can be translated "to men on whom his favor rests" (NIV) or "to people He favors" (HCSB). The emphasis seems to be on God's grace or good will directed to people on earth and expressed in **peace.**

Peace (*eirene*) is the Greek equivalent of the Hebrew *shalom.* Both mean more than the cessation of war, although the promise of the future is that God will cause wars to cease. The emphasis here is on the divine salvation that is brought by the coming of the **Savior.** This includes peace with God (Rom. 5:1), peace with fellow believers (Eph. 2:14), and inner peace that passes human understanding (Phil. 4:7). The celebration of Christmas signifies all these aspects of peace.

Christmas of 1914 was the first Christmas of what was to become the bloodiest war in human history until that time. The horrors of trench warfare already had begun and German troops were fighting the Allied armies of France and Britain. A spontaneous feeling of peace broke out along the trenches, especially in the places where British and German soldiers had been fighting. Each side heard the other singing, and courageous individuals ventured into "no man's land" between the trenches. An informal Christmas truce was agreed to at many points. Each side allowed the other to collect their dead and wounded. Individuals and groups from opposing sides met and exchanged various tokens.

A 25-year-old lieutenant with the Scots Guards, Sir Edward Hulse, wrote in the battalion diary, "Detachments of British and Germans formed a line and a German and English Chaplain read some prayers alternately. The whole of this was done in great solemnity and reverence."[5] When the higher officers of both sides discovered that their troops had ceased slaughtering one another, they angrily ordered the troops back to the fighting. This never happened again in any of the wartime Christmases that followed. The fighting had become too brutal. However, for one Christmas the spirit of peace inherent in the coming of the Prince of peace spread its influence over the battlefront. This is one of the good things about Christmas. It reminds us of the inner peace we have now and gives us hope for the coming of the ultimate peace foretold in Scripture.

Then pealed the bells more loud and deep:
"God is not dead, nor doth He sleep;
The wrong shall fail, the right prevail,
With peace on earth, good will to men."[6]

The Joyous Celebration (Luke 2:15-20)

Verses 15-20: **And it came to pass, as the angels were gone away from them into heaven, the shepherds said one to another, Let us now go even unto Bethlehem, and see this thing which is come to pass, which the Lord hath made known unto us. [16]And they came with haste, and found Mary, and Joseph, and the babe lying in a manger. [17]And when they had seen it, they made known abroad the saying which was told them concerning this child. [18]And all they that heard it wondered at those things which were told them by the shepherds. [19]But Mary kept all these things, and pondered them in her heart. [20]And the shepherds returned, glorifying and praising God for all the things that they had heard and seen, as it was told unto them.**

Shepherd, why did you decide to go and seek the child? "As soon as the angel and the heavenly host left, we all began to talk at once. Each one wanted to go right away and see what the Lord had told us through His angels."

The words **one to another** and **let us** show that the shepherds were all agreed. **Now go** shows that they went quickly. The last part of verse 15 shows that they considered the angels' message what **the Lord** had **made known** to them. The words **they came with haste** also shows how quickly they acted. They are good examples of those who respond quickly to the Word of the Lord.

Shepherd, how did you find the child? "We remembered that the angel had told us that the sign was that He was wrapped in swaddling clothes and lying in a manger. We asked around and the Lord led us to the place. There we found the child, with Mary and Joseph."

Many nativity scenes and Christmas pageants have the wise men also coming to the place of Jesus' birth; however, they came later when the Child was in a house (Matt. 2:11). Thus the shepherds were the first group of outsiders not only to hear the message of Jesus' coming but also to see the newborn King.

Shepherd, why did you tell the people of Bethlehem, and how did they respond? "We had experienced something that we could not keep to ourselves. Therefore, we told everyone we met what the angel had told us and what we had found. The people of Bethlehem showed wonder and amazement at what we told them. I don't know if they themselves went to seek the Savior."

The shepherds added another "first" to their list. They were also the first humans to tell the good news of the coming of Jesus. The words **all they that heard it wondered** ("were amazed," NIV, HCSB; "marveled," NKJV) do not tell us whether their wonder led them to go to where Jesus was and see Him for themselves.

Mary, what was your response to the events of that night? "I was, of course, caught up in the mixed pain and joy of delivering a child. I knew from what the angel had told me and from my own experience that He was more than merely a human child. In light of what happened later, I realize that at the time I did not fully understand the nature of His mission as Savior and what it would cost Him; however, I kept my memories of that special night and pondered them in my heart."

Verse 19 is our source for this answer, along with later references to Mary in the New Testament. Simeon told Mary a few days later that a sword would pierce her soul (v. 35). **Kept** ("treasured," NIV) and **pondered** describe Mary's responses. She remembered all these things, and she spent much time considering the meaning of these events. Many Bible students think that Mary may have been Luke's human source for the intimate events of Luke 1–2.

Shepherd, what were the continuing results of your experiences of that night? "We were never the same after that night. Even as we went back to our work we went with joy and praise to God for what we had seen and heard."

Verse 20 shows that the effect of seeing the Lord ought to be continuing praise and joy. We can apply this to the continuing effects of celebrating the birth of Jesus. This ought not to be confined to one day or season, but should permeate all our days and seasons.

> While by the sheep we watched at night,
> Glad tidings brought an angel bright.

How great our joy! How great our joy!
Joy, joy, joy! Joy, joy, joy!
Praise we the Lord in heav'n on high!
Praise we the Lord in heav'n on high![7]

❖ *Spiritual Transformations*

God used the emperor's decree to have Jesus born in Bethlehem after Joseph and Mary journeyed there. This momentous event divided history. Angels announced the good news of the birth of the Savior, Christ, and Lord to shepherds. The shepherds went quickly to Bethlehem, saw Jesus, told others, and returned glorifying and praising God.

Some people have trouble with the word *celebration.* They fear that it sounds too much like the non-Christian ways of acting during the holiday season. Such sinful partying as is described in Romans 13:11-14 has no place at any season. But Christian joy and peace, praising and glorifying God are appropriate at any season, especially at Christmas.

In what ways do you and your family celebrate Christmas?

_____ Read the Bible story of Jesus' birth from Luke 1–2 and Matthew 1–2
_____ Read other Christmas stories that reflect the spirit of Christmas
_____ Sing and listen to Christmas music
_____ Worship in church
_____ Get together as a family
_____ Give to missions and to other needs
_____ Decorate for Christmas in a manner that honors Christ
_____ Give to people who are less fortunate

Prayer of Commitment: Lord, help me to keep Christ at the center of my celebration of His birth.

[1]Darrell L. Bock, *Luke 1:1–9:50,* in Baker Exegetical Commentary of the New Testament, vol. 3a [Grand Rapids: Baker Book House, 1994], 205.

[2]Robert H. Stein, "Luke," in *The New American Commentary,* vol. 24 [Nashville: Broadman Press, 1992], 107.

[3]Oscar Cullmann, *Christ and Time* [Philadelphia: The Westminster Press, 1950], 17.

[4]Herschel H. Hobbs, *An Exposition of the Gospel of Luke* [Grand Rapids: Baker Book House, 1966], 51.

[5]Martin Gilbert, *The First World War: A Complete History* [New York: Henry Holt and Company, 1994], 117.

[6]Henry Wadsworth Longfellow, "I Heard the Bells on Christmas Day," No. 98, *The Baptist Hymnal,* 1991.

[7]Traditional German carol, "How Great Our Joy," No. 108, *The Baptist Hymnal,* 1991.

THE LOVE OF CHRISTMAS

Bible Passage: John 3:16; 1 John 3:11-24
Key Verse: John 3:16

❖ *Significance of the Lesson*

• The *Theme* of this lesson is that celebrating Christmas includes showing genuine love.

• The *Life Question* this lesson seeks to address is, How can I show love during the Christmas season and throughout the coming year?

• The *Biblical Truth* is that God's great love was expressed supremely in His giving His one and only Son for people's salvation, and people who place their faith in Christ are to love others.

• The *Life Impact* is to help you demonstrate God's kind of love in concrete, practical ways.

What Is Love?

In the secular worldview, the word *love* has many shades of meaning. It can signify intense longing: "I would love to have a condominium on the beach." It can express intense favor or preference—loving luxury cars, ice cream, and good times. It can have the shallow romanticism portrayed in movies and on television. It can be synonymous with sexual lust.

In the biblical worldview, God's love is the standard and source of Christian love. He has expressed His love supremely in Jesus Christ. When we receive His love, He expects us to love Him and others with the same kind of love. Such love is not based on emotions, although genuine affection can be a part of it. God's kind of love is doing what is good for others, regardless of our feelings for them and regardless of the cost to us.

Word Study: *Love*

First-century Greek had several words for *love*. The one most often used of God's love and Christian love is *agapao,* or the noun *agape.* *Agapao* is found in John 3:16 and in 1 John 3:11, 14 (two times), 18, and 23. *Agape* is found in 1 John 3:16. Both the verb and the noun refer to God's kind of love, which is self-giving and sacrificial.

❖ *Search the Scriptures*

God's love in sending Jesus to give His life for sinners is the supreme example of love. Those who experience God's love show it by loving one another, the opposite way from the hatred of the world. Christian love must be put into action in meeting the needs of others. Those who obey God's commandment of love find assurance that opens the way of prayer.

Supreme Example of Love (John 3:16)

Why is John 3:16 probably the most familiar verse in the New Testament? What does it tell us about God's love—its scope, its expression, its purpose, and its desired response?

John 3:16: For God so loved the world, that he gave his only begotten Son, that whosoever believeth in him should not perish, but have everlasting life.

This is a good verse for Christmas and for every season of the year. It clearly states the heart of the Christian good news. Its theme is God's great love. The scope of His love was the whole **world.** This inclusiveness is also seen in the word **whosoever.** The expression and extent of His love was that God **gave his only begotten** ("one and only," NIV) **Son.** The ultimate purpose of His love was that people **should not perish but have everlasting life. Perish** shows the plight of **the world** because of its sin. God's love in sending His **Son** was to save sinners from perishing in their sins; instead, He wanted to give them **everlasting life.** The desired response to His love is that people believe **(believeth).**

This great love is offered to all people, but sinners must believe in Christ to receive the eternal life that God's love makes possible through His Son. Saving faith is more than just giving intellectual assent to the truth of John 3:16. It begins with belief but must include trust and commitment to Christ.

John 3:16 is a powerful text for Christmas because it gives the real significance of the coming of Jesus Christ. We have noted in earlier lessons how Christmas celebrates and expresses hope, joy, and peace. This lesson and passage express and celebrate love—God's love for us in sending His Son and our love for one another.

Love came down at Christmas,
Love all lovely, Love divine;
Love was born at Christmas;
Star and angel gave the sign.

Love shall be our token;
Love be yours and love be mine;
Love to God and all men,
Love for plea and gift and sign.[1]

Decisive Evidence of Love (1 John 3:11-15)

Why did John place such emphasis on loving one another? What sins did Cain exemplify? Is hatred as serious as murder? Why does the world hate believers? How have believers passed from death unto life? Can murderers ever be forgiven?

1 John 3:11-15: For this is the message that ye heard from the beginning, that we should love one another. [12]Not as Cain, who was of that wicked one, and slew his brother. And wherefore slew he him? Because his own works were evil, and his brother's righteous. [13]Marvel not, my brethren, if the world hate you. [14]We know that we have passed from death unto life, because we love the brethren. He that loveth not his brother abideth in death. [15]Whosoever hateth his brother is a murderer: and ye know that no murderer hath eternal life abiding in him.

"This is the first use in the Epistle of the words 'to love one another' (3:23; 4:7,11,12; 2 Jn. 5), but the phrase means exactly the same as 'to love one's brother' (2:10; 3:10,14; 4:20f.)."[2] Jesus had given this as a new commandment to His disciples (John 13:34-35). John earlier called it a new-old commandment (1 John 2:7-8). In one sense, God had always commanded people to love their neighbors (Lev. 19:18). But Christ had created a new bond of love for believers. Thus it is both old and new. At any rate, the Christians to whom John wrote had **heard** this command **from the beginning** of their instruction in the way of Christ.

The opposite way of treating others is epitomized by **Cain.** He did not act as one who belonged to God but rather as one who belonged to **that wicked one** ("the evil one," NIV, HCSB). He **slew** ("murdered," NIV, HCSB) means "to slaughter a victim." Why did Cain murder his brother Abel? John said it was **because his own works were evil, and his**

brother's righteous. Evil is *ponera,* another form of the word used for "the evil one." In verses 8-10 John contrasted the children of God, who are righteous, with sinners, who are of the devil. Jesus said that the devil was a murderer from the beginning (John 8:44). Verse 10 lists among the sins of the devil's children their failure to love their brothers.

John followed Jesus in teaching disciples **not** to **marvel** when **the world** hates them (see John 15:18-19). The world hated Jesus and put Him to death; believers should not be surprised when the same kind of sinful world hates the followers of Christ. Why did Cain murder his brother? He was angered by his **brother's righteous** life.

When we think of murderers such as Cain, we may feel smugly self-righteous because we are not murderers. John's words in verse 15 should destroy such smugness. **Whosoever hateth his brother is a murderer.** This reminds us of the teaching of Jesus in Matthew 5:21-22. Jesus extended the Sixth Commandment to cover anger and verbal abuse.

Verse 14 makes two important points. One is positive. **We know that we have passed from death unto life, because we love the brethren.** This does not mean that our love for others is the basis for our salvation in passing from death unto life. It means that loving others is evidence that we have passed from death unto life. Passing from death unto life pictures the spiritual resurrection of someone dead in sins to new life in Christ (John 5:24; Eph. 2:1-10). One mark of true conversion is brotherly love.

The last part of the verse is sobering. One does not have to be a murderer or filled with hatred to be guilty of serious sin. **He that loveth not his brother abideth in death.** In other words, the opposite of love often is not hatred but indifference. Verses 17-18 deal with this sin in more detail.

Does **no murderer hath eternal life abiding in him** mean that murder is an unpardonable sin? No. God can forgive even a murderer if the person truly repents. John was writing about those who do not seek forgiveness. Of course, even when a murderer is forgiven, the person must live with the earthly consequences of this terrible sin.

Thus loving one another is one of the decisive evidences of Christian love. Hatred and indifference are evidences of lack of real faith and love. What are the evidences for keeping Christmas in a Christian way? Acts of love for church, for family, for friends, and for the needy show Christian love.

Practical Expression of Love (1 John 3:16-20)

How do we know what love is? How is God's love distinctive? How does experiencing God's love obligate us? Why must Christians give worldly possessions to those in need? How do words express love? Why must love include more than words? How can believers know they are of the truth? How can believers handle times of having a guilty conscience?

1 John 3:16: Hereby perceive we the love of God, because he laid down his life for us: and we ought to lay down our lives for the brethren.

Christians **perceive** God's **love.** The words **of God** are not in the Greek text. Literally it reads, "By this we know love" (NKJV). This could refer to the love of God the Father or God the Son. We know God's love because He sent His Son into the world to be the sacrifice for our sins and the Savior from our sins (4:10,14). This verse stresses the reality of Christ's death, that **he laid down his life for us.** God sent His Son to die not for friends, but because people were sinners and separated from God. He showed His great love in dying for us while we were yet sinners (Rom. 5:6-8).

Because He **laid down his life for us . . . we ought to lay down our lives for the brethren.** Giving one's life for others is the most that anyone can give. Under persecution, this kind of total self-giving sometimes took place—and still takes place around this world. Lesser but equally real forms of Christian love call for doing good for one another, especially when someone is in need.

1 John 3:17-18: But whoso hath this world's good, and seeth his brother have need, and shutteth up his bowels of compassion from him, how dwelleth the love of God in him? [18]My little children, let us not love in word, neither in tongue; but in deed and in truth.

Christian love is basically an action. One of the practical expressions of Christian love is sharing our means of living with those in need. **This world's good** ("material possessions," NIV) translates *bion tou kosmou,* "life's possessions of the world." This reminds us that what we have is what life has been invested into acquiring. This word is used in Luke 15:12,30 of the property or means of living provided to the prodigal son by his father. This is also the word used of the amount given by the poor widow in the temple (Mark 12:44). **Need** refers to a real need, not just something someone wants. **Shutteth up his bowels of compassion** includes the word for "lock" or "shut" and the word for internal organs. The latter word reflects the belief in ancient times that the internal organs were the source of human emotions. Thus it may be translated using modern terms as "shuts up his heart" (NKJV).

John's question about the one who closes his heart to the needs of a **brother** is, **how dwelleth the love of God in him?** ("How can the love of God be in him?" NIV.) He sees the need but does nothing to help. Verse 18 says that he may say something, but if he does nothing, his words are empty. The point of verse 18 is that our actions should back up our words. Words of love need to be accompanied by deeds of love.

In describing the love shown by the early Christians, Aristides wrote to the Roman emperor Hadrian: "They love one another. They never fail to help widows; they save orphans from those who will hurt them. If they have something, they give freely to the man who has nothing; if they see a stranger, they take him home and are happy, as though he were a real brother. They don't consider themselves brothers and sisters in the usual sense, but brothers instead through the Spirit, in God."[3]

1 John 3:19-20: **And hereby we know that we are of the truth, and shall assure our hearts before him.** [20]**For if our heart condemn us, God is greater than our heart, and knoweth all things.**

These are two of the most difficult verses to translate. The first problem is whether **hereby** refers to what precedes or to what follows. Many Bible students think it refers to what preceded it. If so, it has a similar meaning to verse 14. That is, one evidence of genuine faith is our love for one another. Another problem is the meaning of the word translated **shall assure** (*peisomen*). It often means "persuade," but at times it means "set at rest." Many Bible students favor the latter meaning. Another difficulty is that the connecting word *hoti* occurs three times. In the *King James Version* it is rendered only twice, as **that** and as **for.** It also could be rendered "because" or "whenever."

Even with these differences, some truths seem clear: (1) Loving acts toward one another are evidences that we belong to the truth. (2) This brings assurance that enables us to set our hearts and consciences at ease. (3) When we do have doubts, the awareness that God knows everything should bring assurance. For a lost person, the awareness that God knows everything is disturbing, but for a believer it is reassuring.

Divine Command to Love (1 John 3:21-24)

How does assurance encourage prayer? Under what conditions does God give us anything we ask for? How can love and faith be commanded? What is involved in abiding in Christ? What is the role of the Spirit in assurance, love, and prayer?

1 John 3:21-24: Beloved, if our heart condemn us not, then have we confidence toward God. ²²And whatsoever we ask, we receive of him, because we keep his commandments, and do those things that are pleasing in his sight. ²³And this is his commandment, That we should believe on the name of his Son Jesus Christ, and love one another, as he gave us commandment. ²⁴And he that keepeth his commandments dwelleth in him, and he in him. And hereby we know that he abideth in us, by the Spirit which he hath given us.

One of the wonderful fruits of assurance **(if our heart condemn us not)** is the boldness with which we can come to God in prayer. **Confidence** is *parresian.* This word has a rich heritage. In ancient Athens it referred to the right of any citizen to speak his mind. In the New Testament it referred to boldness in witnessing and in prayer. This **confidence** enables us to "come boldly unto the throne of grace, that we may obtain mercy, and find grace to help in time of need (Heb. 4:16). John promised that **whatsoever we ask, we receive of him.** John R. W. Stott observed: "This simple and unqualified promise must, of course, be interpreted in the light of further conditions upon which, in other parts of Scripture, God promises to grant his people's requests. If a prayer is to be answered it must be 'according to his will' (5:14; cf. Ps. 37:4; John 15:7)."[4]

This promise is possible **because we keep his commandments, and do those things that are pleasing in his sight.** Herschel H. Hobbs pointed out that this is another way of saying that "our wills will be blended perfectly with His will. Therefore, we will ask for nothing which is outside His will."[5]

John then spelled out two of these commandments: **Believe on the name of his Son Jesus Christ, and love one another.** Someone may ask, How can such things be commanded? The answer is that both are the results of acts of will. We decide whether to commit ourselves to Christ and whether to act in love.

Involved in obeying these commandments is that we abide in Christ and He abides in us. And how do **we know that he abideth in us**? We know **by the Spirit which he hath given us.** John goes on in 4:1-6 to describe how to know whether we are being led by His Spirit or by some other spirit. The clue is whether the Spirit leads us to live like Jesus. If not, it is not His Spirit.

❖ *Spiritual Transformations*

God's great love was revealed in sending His only Son so that people might not perish but have everlasting life. A decisive evidence of a proper response to this love is for Christians to love one another. Genuine Christian love acts for the good of others. Assurance enables believers to come boldly to God's throne of grace in prayer. Obeying God's commandments is possible by the Spirit who abides in us.

Christmas is an ideal time to speak words of love and to do acts of love. This is the time for the Lottie Moon Christmas Offering for International Missions. An awareness of the deep physical and spiritual needs in other lands motivates believers to use this offering as a means for helping to meet these needs.

Christmas is also a time for helping to meet the needs in our own communities. All kinds of opportunities for gifts and service are available in most communities.

Christmas is a time for renewing our love for one another in our churches. Many people who come to church are looking for the very things that Christ offers—life, love, hope, joy, and peace. Some have never trusted Christ. Others have been beaten down by the troubles of life. An especially needy group are those who have lost loved ones during the previous year. Since Christmas is such a family time, they miss their loved ones most intensely at Christmas.

Christmas is a family time. This is one of its good features. Thus it is an ideal occasion for mending strained or broken relations. And it is a time for expressing with words and actions our love and affirmation of others.

Which of these practical expressions of love for others have you done or will you do this Christmas? _____

Prayer of Commitment: Lord, guide and empower me to act in Your love at this season and at all times.

[1]Christina G. Rossetti, "Love Came Down at Christmas," No. 109, *The Baptist Hymnal*, 1991.

[2]I. Howard Marshall, *The Epistles of John*, in The New International Commentary on the New Testament [Grand Rapids: William B. Eerdmans Publishing Company, 1978], 189.

[3]Quoted in Roy B. Zuck, *The Speaker's Quote Book* [Grand Rapids: Kregel Publications, 1997], 234.

[4]John R. W. Stott, *The Letters of John*, rev. ed., in the Tyndale New Testament Commentaries [Grand Rapids: William B. Eerdmans Publishing Company, 1988], 153.

[5]Herschel H. Hobbs, *The Epistles of John* [Nashville: Thomas Nelson Publishers, 1983], 94.

THE CHALLENGE OF CHRISTMAS

Background Passage: Philippians 3:1–4:1
Focal Passage: Philippians 3:1-14
Key Verses: Philippians 3:7-8

❖ *Significance of the Lesson*

• The *Theme* of this lesson is that Jesus is more important than anything else.
• The *Life Question* this lesson seeks to address is, How can I show that Jesus is more important to me than anything else?
• The *Biblical Truth* is that knowing Jesus as Lord is life's highest priority.
• The *Life Impact* is to help you make Jesus most important in your life.

Jesus' Place in the Lives of Adults

In the secular worldview, Jesus is not important or He is no more important than any other moral and religious teacher of history. Experiencing a personal relationship with Him has no place in people's lives. Making Him Lord is not part of the secular view.

In the biblical worldview, Jesus is supremely important in history and in the lives of believers. He is given continuing priority in their lives. No one else or nothing else is allowed to take His place of ultimate importance.

Paul's Letter to the Philippians

Paul's missionary work in Philippi is described in Acts 16:12-40. His continuing relationship with them is reflected in his letter to them. He was under house arrest in Rome at the time, and the Philippian church had sent him money and one of their members to help him. Paul wrote for several reasons: (1) to reassure them that God was using his imprisonment for good, (2) to call on them to rejoice with him in the

Lord, (3) to urge them to be one in spirit, (4) to thank them for being good news partners with him, and (5) to warn them against false teachers. In the process Paul revealed much about himself.

Word Study: *Gain, Loss*

In Philippians 3:7 Paul used the language of accounting to describe the contrast between what he at one time considered profit and loss and what he considered profit and loss after coming to know Christ. The word for "profit" (NIV) or **gain** is *kerdos*; and the word for **loss** is *zemia*. The basic meaning of these two words is "advantage" and "disadvantage." The verb form of each of these is found in verse 8.

❖ *Search the Scriptures*

Paul warned against those whose confidence is in their own achievements and told how he once had felt that way. He told how he counted all such achievements as loss for the supreme glory of knowing Christ. Paul made clear that he was not perfect, but he testified that he was pressing on toward God's purpose for his life.

Glorying in Christ (Phil. 3:1-6)

How can we explain the sudden change in tone between verses 1 and 2? Against what group was Paul warning the Philippians in verse 2? What did Paul mean by **confidence in the flesh**? *In what sense did he "glory" in Christ? What examples of his own confidence in the flesh did Paul mention? How did Paul change his views of what was* **gain** *and what was* **loss**? *How could Paul consider his persecution of the church to be a mark of religious zeal?* These questions are addressed in comments on these verses.

Verses 1-3: Finally, my brethren, rejoice in the Lord. To write the same things to you, to me indeed is not grievous, but for you it is safe. [2]Beware of dogs, beware of evil workers, beware of the concision. [3]For we are the circumcision, which worship God in the spirit, and rejoice in Christ Jesus, and have no confidence in the flesh.

Finally is literally "as for the rest." The Greek *to loipon* sometimes means "finally," but it also can mean "in addition." At times Paul used it as a conclusion (2 Cor. 13:11), and at other times he used it as a transition (1 Thess. 4:1).

What did Paul mean by **the same things**? One possibility is that he was writing about something that he already had written in this letter. It might have been his call for them to rejoice. Another possibility is that he was thinking of previous warnings against false teachers. Whatever it was, Paul said that writing them was **not grievous** ("tedious," NKJV; "troublesome," NRSV) to him because it was a "safeguard" (NIV) for them. **Rejoice in the Lord** is a key theme in Philippians.

What caused Paul to suddenly leave this positive theme and issue such a strongly worded warning against **dogs**? In ancient society dogs were considered wild and vicious animals. The Jews sometimes referred to Gentiles as dogs. Apparently Paul wanted to contrast the joy of believers with the deadly danger posed by those who placed their **confidence in the flesh.**

Verse 2 is a strong warning against people whom Paul considered dangerous. He used the word *blepete* three times to warn them to **beware** of some group whom he described as **dogs . . . evil workers . . . the concision.** The last term translates *katatomen*, which means "to cut to pieces" or "mutilate." Hence "those who mutilate the flesh" (NRSV, HCSB). This is contrasted with *peritome*, which means **circumcision** or "to cut around." Paul seems to have been using this play on words to show his contempt for the Judaizers, who were insisting that Gentile believers must be circumcised to be saved.

Paul reminded the believers in Philippi—Jews and Gentiles—that he and they were **the circumcision.** Elsewhere he spoke of the difference between circumcision of the flesh and an inward circumcision (Rom. 2:29; 3:30; Gal. 6:12-13). This is another way of insisting that salvation is by grace through faith for Jews and for Gentiles. Those who have the circumcision of the heart are the true people of God, not those who trust in their physical circumcision and keeping of the Jewish law. Paul listed three characteristics of the true people of God. (1) They **worship God in the spirit** ("Spirit," NKJV, NIV, NRSV, HCSB). (2) They **rejoice in Christ Jesus. Rejoice** here is a different word from the word for **rejoice** in verse 1. This word in verse 3 can be translated "glory" (NIV) or "boast" (NRSV, HCSB). (3) They **have no confidence in the flesh.**

Flesh was used by Paul at times to refer to the fleshy part of a body. However, his normal use of the word described people who were living on their own, not by the Spirit of God. The sins of the flesh were more than sensual sins. Life in the flesh means living on our own resources, in contrast to life in the Spirit. **Confidence in the flesh,** therefore, means to rely on the flesh instead of on God.

The Judaizers had placed their confidence in their own achievements and religious rituals, not in God and His grace. Paul's opponents would have strongly disagreed that they were living like nonbelievers. They considered themselves deeply spiritual, devoutly religious, and highly moral people. But Paul was accusing them of placing their confidence in the flesh because of their preoccupation with heritage, rituals, and laws. These things led to trusting themselves rather than trusting God. As an illustration of what he meant by **confidence in the flesh,** Paul cited his own life before he became a Christian.

Verses 4-6: **Though I might also have confidence in the flesh. If any other man thinketh that he hath whereof he might trust in the flesh, I more: ⁵Circumcised the eighth day, of the stock of Israel, of the tribe of Benjamin, an Hebrew of the Hebrews; as touching the law, a Pharisee; ⁶concerning zeal, persecuting the church; touching the righteousness which is in the law, blameless.**

Paul had once thought much like the Judaizers. He said that if it came to a boasting contest about the things in which they trusted, he could more than hold his own. "If anyone else thinks he has reasons to put confidence in the flesh, I have more" (NIV). With these words of introduction, Paul described his old life. He revealed some valuable facts about his former life and outlook. He mentioned four aspects of his rich Jewish heritage and three areas in which he exercised his own choices.

Circumcision was a big thing with the Judaizers. Paul was **circumcised the eighth day,** according to the Jewish law. He was **of the stock** ("people," NIV; "nation," HCSB) **of Israel.** He was not someone who came to the Jewish faith from the outside. He and his family had maintained their tribal identity. He was **of the tribe of Benjamin.** Although Paul grew up outside the holy land, he had maintained his strong Jewish identity amid all the temptations of the Gentile culture. He was **an Hebrew of the Hebrews.** These four things emphasized his right to claim the full benefits of being Jewish.

When Saul of Tarsus was old enough, he became **a Pharisee.** Paul mentioned **the law** because of the Pharisees' fanatical adherence to the letter of the law. The strength of his religious **zeal** was seen in his

persecuting the church. When he measured himself by **the righteousness which is in the law,** Saul considered himself **blameless.**

How could a decent man consider persecuting others a sign of moral and spiritual zeal? Like many persecutors down through history, Paul felt he was serving God by imprisoning and putting to death people of another religion. Why did Paul list persecution along with the other examples of confidence in the flesh? He wanted all to realize that confidence in our own achievements can include some things that are not real achievements at all; instead, they are acts of evil.

The Judaizers and the Pharisees were examples of religious people whose real confidence was not in God and His grace but in themselves—their religious practices and righteous lives. The Bible defines sin as anything that separates people from God. Religion and righteousness (actually self-righteousness) can become our deadliest sins. The self-righteous person is separated from God by his or her supposed righteousness.

Paul by contrast lived a life that was centered in Jesus Christ. He wrote, "For to me to live is Christ" (1:21), and "I can do all things through Christ which strengtheneth me" (4:13). As we see here in 3:3, Paul gloried or boasted in Christ, which is another way of saying that his confidence was in Christ.

Making Christ Life's Priority (Phil. 3:7-11)

How did Paul use the language of accounting to contrast his old life and his new life in Christ? How do his words keep the focus on Christ? Was Paul focused on his past, present, or future life? What did he say about **righteousness**? If Paul already knew Christ, why did he write that his goal was to **know him**? How did Paul hope to share in Christ's **sufferings** and **death**? Does the last part of verse 11 indicate some doubt by Paul about sharing in the future resurrection?

Verses 7-8: **But what things were gain to me, those I counted loss for Christ. ⁸Yea doubtless, and I count all things but loss for the excellency of the knowledge of Christ Jesus my Lord: for whom I have suffered the loss of all things, and do count them but dung, that I may win Christ.**

Verse 7 states Paul's change from confidence in the flesh to confidence in Christ. He used accounting terms to describe the **things** in which he had trusted as **gain** ("gains," NRSV; "profit," NIV). That is, before the Damascus road experience, he considered them as his greatest advantages. But now he wrote, **those I counted loss for Christ. Counted** ("have counted," NASB) is *hegemai,* which is in the perfect tense and refers to what had a beginning point and continues to the present time. He was thinking of the reappraisal of his life after he encountered Christ. Those things in which he once trusted and considered his greatest treasures, he considered as losses for the sake of Christ. He added up all the things mentioned in verses 5-6—things that he had placed on the credit or profit side of the ledger of his life— and realized that they actually belonged on the debit side of the ledger.

Verse 8 intensifies verse 7 and brings it into the present. **Count** is *hegoumai,* which is present tense. Paul was saying that he still felt that way only more so. He had referred to **things** in verse 7; he referred to **all things** in verse 8. The most important intensification is in the words **for the excellency** ("surpassing greatness," NIV; "surpassing value," NRSV, HCSB) **of the knowledge of Christ Jesus my Lord.** These words remind us of the parables of the hidden treasure and the pearl of great price. Jesus told these brief parables to illustrate the surpassing value of the kingdom of heaven. When the man who was plowing found the treasure, he sold everything to get that treasure. When the merchant found the pearl, he did the same thing (Matt. 13:44-46). The longer Paul knew Christ, the more he realized the surpassing value of this relationship.

Verse 8 gives yet another intensification. Paul considered the old life not only as a loss, but he considered it as **dung** ("rubbish," NIV, NRSV, NKJV; "filth," HCSB). What he had found in Christ was so much better; he realized all his former achievements of self were like so much useless garbage. Many non-Christians refrain from becoming Christians because they think they will have to give up too much. That sounds foolish to mature Christians. We realize that Jesus asks us to give up slavery, disease, and death for freedom, health, and life.

The final part of verse 8 sets the stage for verse 9. Paul **suffered the loss of all things** that he might **win** ("gain," NIV, HCSB, NRSV, NKJV) **Christ. May win** ("may gain," NIV, HCSB, NRSV, NKJV) is in the subjunctive mood, which has an implication that the fulfillment of it was still in the future.

Verses 9-11: **And be found in him, not having mine own righteousness, which is of the law, but that which is through the faith**

of Christ, the righteousness which is of God by faith: [10]**that I may know him, and the power of his resurrection, and the fellowship of his sufferings, being made conformable unto his death;** [11]**if by any means I might attain unto the resurrection of the dead.**

Be found translates another verb in the subjunctive mood. It also has this unfulfilled dimension to it. In fact, verses 9-11 illustrate what Gordon D. Fee called the "already but not yet" perspective of Paul's faith and experience.[1] This same perspective explains why Paul wrote **that I may know him.** Paul knew Christ because of what He had done for him, but Paul's ultimate goal was to have his present knowledge of Christ fully realized in the resurrection. The entire context of verses 8-11 has this tension between present reality and future fulfillment. "What we have in Christ is already real and precious, but this reality holds in prospect a fulfillment even more wonderful than anything we have yet experienced. On the one hand, Paul already had gained Christ, was already found in him, and already knew him. On the other hand, gaining Christ, being found in him, and knowing him in the fullest sense were yet future."[2]

Nearly all of Paul's great words and ideas had this futuristic cast to them. One of his key words was **righteousness.** Paul taught that people are sinners who need to be made right with God. The Pharisees taught that people could become right with God by their good lives and religious devotion. Paul insisted that sinners can be set right with God only by His grace, on the basis of the death of Christ, and on condition of faith in Christ. These ideas lie in the background of verse 9. Paul contrasted the two views of righteousness. The Judaizers had the view that Paul once held. But now Paul did not trust in his **own righteousness, which is of the law.** Instead, he trusted **the righteousness . . . which is through the faith of** ("in," NIV, HCSB, NKJV) **Christ, the righteousness which is of** ("from," NIV, HCSB, NKJV) **God by faith.**

Paul's view of knowing Christ also has a present-future tone. Obviously he already knew Christ. He wrote, "I know whom I have believed, and am persuaded that he is able to keep that which I have committed to him against that day" (2 Tim. 1:12). Notice four things about what Paul meant by knowing Christ. (1) He meant that he knew Christ personally, not just knew things about Him. (2) The better he knew Christ, the better he wanted to know Him. (3) He had confident hope of knowing Him better in the future. (4) Wanting to know Christ better motivated him to seek to become more like Him.

Knowing Christ involves a desire to know **the power of his resurrection, and the fellowship of his sufferings.** These are inseparable experiences. To know **the power of his resurrection** is based on two past realities and includes one present and one future reality. The past realities are the resurrection of Jesus Christ from the dead and the spiritual resurrection of a new believer from being dead in sins to being alive in Jesus Christ. The present reality was Paul's desire to live in the power of the resurrection. He wrote to the Ephesians that believers had power to live the Christian life that was equal to the power that raised Jesus from the dead (Eph. 1:19-20). This power comes to believers through the Spirit of the crucified-resurrected Lord. The future reality was the future resurrection of believers in the end time.

The fellowship of his sufferings uses the word *koinonian*, which means "to share in" or "to participate in" something. It is "the fellowship of sharing in His sufferings" (NIV). This does not refer to sharing in sufferings that help to atone for the sins of the world but to the sufferings that come to those who faithfully follow the Lord in the way of the cross. As Paul put it earlier in this letter, "For unto you it is given in the behalf of Christ, not only to believe on him, but also to suffer for his sake" (1:29).

The result of the Christian's experience of the cross is **being made conformable unto his death.** This means that the power of God works in our lives to create what we cannot do ourselves—help us to live by the way of the cross. The cross and resurrection of Jesus provide not only the door to the Christian life but also to the way of the Christian life. This is what Jesus meant when He spoke of the necessity of taking up one's cross to follow Him. Believers are not only to come to Christ by way of the cross, but the cross is to become our way of living. Living by the way of the cross involves denying ourselves and putting God and others first. This cannot be done in our own strength but only in **the power of his resurrection.** The Spirit of the crucified, risen Lord within us enables believers to walk the way of agape love. Elsewhere Paul expressed it like this: "I am crucified with Christ: nevertheless I live; yet not I, but Christ liveth in me: and the life which I now live in the flesh I live by the faith of the Son of God, who loved me, and gave himself for me" (Gal. 2:20).

Verse 11 puzzles many Bible students. Paul, who elsewhere was so confident of his future resurrection in Christ, seemed to express uncertainty about it. He wrote, **if by any means** ("somehow," NIV) **I might**

attain unto the resurrection of the dead. Because he was elsewhere so confident of this, we can assume that he was not expressing doubt about it. What then was he saying? He obviously was leading into verses 12-14, which do not express uncertainty but emphasize pressing on rather than being complacent. Paul may have simply been refuting any notion that he had already attained all these things about which he had written in verses 9-11. Another factor may have been a group in Philippi who claimed to be perfect and to have already arrived. We know that there was a group in the first century who claimed that their own resurrection was past (2 Tim. 2:18). Paul wanted them to know that the realization of the Christian hope was still in the future, and that we should not boast of having already attained all we need.

Moving Toward God's Goal (Phil. 3:12-14)

What is the relationship between verses 12-14 and the preceding verses? Why did Paul deny having been perfected? What is the meaning of **follow after**? *What is meant by* **apprehended**? *What things did Paul forget? How is the Christian life like a race?*

Verses 12-14: Not as though I had already attained, either were already perfect: but I follow after, if that I may apprehend that for which also I am apprehended of Christ Jesus. [13]Brethren, I count not myself to have apprehended: but this one thing I do, forgetting those things which are behind, and reaching forth unto those things which are before, [14]I press toward the mark for the prize of the high calling of God in Christ Jesus.

In looking at verses 12-14 we face the same question asked about the meaning of verse 11. Why did Paul make so much of the fact that he had **not . . . already attained**? **Attained** translates *elabon,* which means "received" or "obtained" (NIV). He also insisted that he was **not . . . already perfect.** This verb is *teteleiomai,* which is in the perfect tense and the passive voice. Thus it does not refer to Paul becoming perfect but to God's bringing him to God's goal for his life. The word does not stress moral perfection so much as reaching a goal.

As we have already noted, some Bible students think that there was a group in Philippi who were claiming to be perfect and to have already arrived. There certainly are people today who claim to be perfect. If Paul denied being perfect, who are we to claim that we have attained what he had not attained? Many professing Christians do not claim to be perfect, but they are content to stop their Christian pilgrimage at some point and become complacent. This achieves the same deadly result as claiming to be perfect. In both cases the person fails to press on in the Christian life.

Follow after in verse 12 is the same word translated **press toward** in verse 14. Its literal meaning is "to pursue." It was used of Paul's persecuting in verse 6, because persecution involves pursuing people. Paul had gone from pursuing Christians for the purpose of punishing them to pursuing God's goal for him.

Apprehend or **apprehended** appear three times in verses 12-13. These translate some form of the word that means to "lay hold on" or to "grasp." "I press on to take hold of that for which Christ Jesus took hold of me" (NIV). God had grasped Paul and given him a new life, purpose, and hope. Paul had not yet grasped the final goal God had for him, but he was pressing on. "Brothers, I do not consider myself yet to have taken hold of it" (NIV).

Paul used the analogy of an athlete running a race. Such an athlete must learn to do four things: (1) Do not allow anything to distract. Thus Paul was not looking back over his shoulder. He was **forgetting those things which are behind.** (2) Concentrate fully on running the race. Thus Paul focused on that **one thing.** (3) Give it all you have. **Reaching forth** is a word meaning "straining forward." (4) Persevere and don't give up. This is emphasized in the word **press toward.**

The words **forgetting those things which are behind** may simply be a way of stressing the need not to be distracted in the Christian race. However, some Bible students seek to identify what kinds of things Paul was seeking to forget. Paul could have been thinking of the guilt of his years of sin (see vv. 4-6). Or he could have been thinking of past accomplishments that the Lord had done through him. "Both the nostalgia of the former life and the 'good ole days' of his Christian life would paralyze him in terms of what God wanted in the future."[3] Too many believers are content to rest on their laurels. They feel they have done all they need to do for the Lord. Only the Lord can tell us when that time has come by calling us home. My prayer is, "Lord, help us to use what health and strength and days You give us in doing what You want us to do."

Verse 14 is a summary of the main points in the passage. Paul was like a racer bearing down on the goal or finish line. He had referred to his goal as that for which the Lord had laid hold of him. Here he called it **the high** ("upward," NASB; "heavenly," NRSV, HCSB) **calling of God in Christ Jesus.** Each Christian has one calling, although God leads us to achieve it in distinctive ways. We all are called to follow Christ in the way of the cross and resurrection. Paul was pressing on toward that goal.

> I'm pressing on the upward way,
> New heights I'm gaining ev'ry day;
> Still praying as I onward bound,
> "Lord, plant my feet on higher ground."[4]

❖ *Spiritual Transformations*

Paul as a Christian gloried in Christ, but he had once placed his confidence in the flesh. He compared what he once thought were gains and found them as losses compared to what he had found and would still find in Christ. He had not yet attained all that God wanted him to be, but he was pressing on.

Those who trust in themselves and human resources miss the only true source for confidence—Christ. Those who are in Christ have found life's greatest treasure. The better believers know Christ the better they want to know him. The Christian life is like a race in which we press on toward God's goal for our lives.

At what points does Paul's experience convict you or challenge you?

_____

What commitments to make Christ central in your life are you making as you prepare for a new year? _____

Prayer of Commitment: Lord Jesus, help me to make You central in all aspects of my life.

[1]Gordon D. Fee, *Paul's Letter to the Philippians*, in The New International Commentary on the New Testament [Grand Rapids: William B. Eerdmans Publishing Company, 1995], 320.

[2]Robert J. Dean, *Philippians: Life at Its Best* [Nashville: Broadman Press, 1980], 96.

[3]Richard R. Melick, Jr., "Philippians, Colossians, Philemon," in *The New American Commentary*, vol. 32 [Nashville: Broadman Press, 1991], 139.

[4]Johnson Oatman, Jr., "Higher Ground," No. 484, in *The Baptist Hymnal*, 1991.

Study Theme

Transformed Attitudes

William James wrote, "The greatest discovery of my generation is that human beings can alter their lives by altering their attitudes of mind."[1] This important insight is consistent with biblical teachings, with one major addition. Christ alone enables us to have our attitudes and actions transformed.

This eight-session study theme focuses on the power of Christ to transform the attitudes and behavior of believers. The studies will explore Bible passages that relate to specific changes. The lesson titles present a negative attitude and the positive attitude to which it is changed.

"Inaction to Action" shows how Christ transforms inactivity to Christ-like actions. "Enemy to Advocate," based on the account of Paul's conversion, shows how Christ changed a persecutor into a strong advocate for Christ. "Devalued to Valued," based on the story of the deliverance of the Hebrew boy babies from Pharaoh, is for Sanctity of Human Life Sunday. "Useless to Useful," based on the appeal of Paul for Onesimus, shows how Christ changes a useless person into a useful one to God and others. "Disrespect to Respect" shows how Christ transforms disrespect for God and others into reverence and respect. "Prejudice to Acceptance" shows how Christ changes prejudice to acceptance and helps believers resist prejudices wherever they find them. "Coveting to Contentment," shows how Christ transforms covetous people into people contented with what they have. "Stockpiling to Sharing" contrasts the stockpiling of the rich farmer with the sacrificial giving of the poor widow.

The Life Impacts of the eight sessions are designed to help you—
- demonstrate your faith by right actions (Jan. 6)
- continue to let Jesus transform your life (Jan. 13)
- value and protect human life (Jan. 20)
- see and affirm others' usefulness in the kingdom of God (Jan. 27)
- respect people and reverence Christ (Feb. 3)
- overcome your prejudices and resist prejudices where you find them (Feb. 10)
- find your contentment in Christ (Feb. 17)
- be a sharing person (Feb. 24)

[1]Zuck, *The Speaker's Quote Book*, 23.

Week of January 6

INACTION TO ACTION

Background Passage: Acts 6:1-7; James 1:22-27; 2:14-18
Focal Passage: Acts 6:1-4; James 1:22-27; 2:14-18
Key Verse: James 2:17

❖ *Significance of the Lesson*

• The *Theme* for this lesson is that Christ in you moves you from inaction to action.
• The *Life Question* this lesson seeks to address is, How do I demonstrate my faith in Christ?
• The *Biblical Truth* is that faith in Christ is demonstrated by right actions.
• The *Life Impact* is to help you demonstrate your faith by right actions.

Religious Faith and Right Actions

In the secular worldview, faith and actions can be separated. Religion can have little or nothing to do with how a person lives. Life is compartmentalized, enabling adults to profess religious faith and participate in religious services and activities while ignoring life's moral and social demands.

In the biblical worldview, faith is the way of salvation; however, when faith is genuine, the result is an impact on how people think and act. Right actions do not save, but they demonstrate the reality of faith.

Widows in the Bible

In Bible times widows were dependent on others for protection and provision. They often were listed with orphans as helpless members of society. Unscrupulous people exploited them. This was a serious sin (Ex. 22:22; Luke 20:47). People of true faith defended the widows against oppression (Isa. 1:17). God had compassion on widows (Deut. 10:18; Luke 7:11-15).

Widows' families were responsible for their care; failing to care for a widowed mother was a serious sin (1 Tim. 5:3-8). In Hebrew society, if there was no living son, the next of kin was responsible (see Ruth 4:13-15). All of the religious community had some responsibilities. In Old Testament times, widows were allowed to glean, and part of the tithes was used to feed them (Deut. 14:24-29; 26:12-13). In New Testament times, the church helped widows whose families were not able to do so (Acts 6:1; 1 Tim. 5:3-16).

Word Study: *Religious, Religion*

The words *religious* and *religion* are found in James 1:26-27. The words themselves do not refer exclusively to Christianity. They referred to any religion or worship of a god. James, of course, was using them of the Christian religion. Many pagan religions made no moral demands of their adherents, but the Christian faith calls for Christian living.

❖ *Search the Scriptures*

Rather than remain inactive in the face of complaints from the Greek-speaking widows regarding equal distribution of food, the Jerusalem church took action to resolve the problem. James insisted that hearing the Word of God involves doing the Word. He emphasized that genuine religion controls the tongue, helps widows and orphans, and is unspotted by the world. He said that faith without works is dead; only faith that works is true faith.

Neglect and Responsibility (Acts 6:1-4)

Why does a growing church often face potential dissension? Who were the two groups of widows in the Jerusalem church? Who made the complaint and why? How was the complaint handled? What is meant by **serve tables***? What were the qualifications for the men who were to be selected?* These questions are addressed by comments on these verses.

Acts 6:1: And in those days, when the number of the disciples was multiplied, there arose a murmuring of the Grecians against the Hebrews, because their widows were neglected in the daily ministration.

During the early days in the Jerusalem church, the church grew in numbers. The best problems for a church are "growing pains." Such problems, however, can be deadly if they are not dealt with in the right way. A growing church brings in more people and usually more diverse groups of people. For example, in the Jerusalem church were two groups of widows. **Grecians** ("Grecian Jews," NIV; "Hellenistic Jews," HCSB) were not Greeks but Jews who spoke Greek and who usually had lived for a while in the Jewish dispersion throughout the ancient world. Many of them now lived in Jerusalem. Some of them may have stayed there after coming for the day of Pentecost (see Acts 2:8-11). **Hebrews** ("Hebraic Jews," NIV, HCSB) were Aramaic-speaking Jews who had grown up in the holy land. Two historical facts explain this difference. The conquests of Alexander the Great had spread Greek language and culture over the ancient world. Greek became the universal language. The other fact was the movement of Jews into all nations. This began with the exile in 586 B.C., but it continued so that by the first-century Jews lived in nearly every city. These Jews spoke Greek, although some, such as Saul of Tarsus, also knew Aramaic. Aramaic was a form of Semitic language spoken by the common people in the holy land. Thus there were differences in language and culture between these two groups.

Widows were dependent on others for help in ancient society. The Old Testament has many passages devoted to the need for the people of God to care for the widows among them. The Jewish believers continued this practice in the early church. The Jerusalem church had set out to try to see that everyone in need was helped (Acts 2:44-45; 4:32-35). The widows were of special concern because they often had real needs. Thus the church had committed itself to distribute food (or money) to them. This was the **daily ministration** ("distribution," NIV, HCSB).

Greek-speaking church members murmured against the Aramaic-speaking members. Actually, the complaint was against those in charge of distributing the food. The complaint was that the Greek-speaking widows were being **neglected in the daily ministration.** **Neglected** means "being overlooked" (NIV, HCSB). Apparently they were not being deliberately shunned; they simply were being overlooked. Apparently the complaint had some basis in fact. It was not just someone grumbling about something unimportant. Food was important. Fairness in distributing it was essential. Wise church leaders listened to the complaints and took action.

Acts 6:2-4: Then the twelve called the multitude of the disciples unto them, and said, It is not reason that we should leave the word of God, and serve tables. [3]Wherefore, brethren, look ye out among you seven men of honest report, full of the Holy Ghost and wisdom, whom we may appoint over this business. [4]But we will give ourselves continually to prayer, and to the ministry of the word.

The twelve here refers to the apostles. **Disciples** in this passage refers to the believers, who were not called Christians until 11:26 in Antioch. The **disciples** were also called **brethren.** The apostles had been in charge of the sharing of material possessions in 4:37. They may have turned this duty over to others, but the others were probably Aramaic-speaking believers like the apostles themselves.

The apostles wisely did not allow the situation to continue once it was brought to their attention. They called together **the multitude** ("all," NIV) **of the disciples.** The apostles began by saying that it was not right for them to **leave the word of God, and serve tables.** They were responsible for seeing that this was done, but they felt they were not the ones to do it. **Serve tables** probably referred to tables on which the food was laid. However, some Bible students think it referred to distribution of money, which the widows in turn used to buy food.

The apostles suggested that the church members select from among them **seven men**, whom the apostles would **appoint over this business** ("appoint to this duty," HCSB; "turn this responsibility over to them," NIV). This action then would free the twelve to concentrate on **prayer** and **the ministry of the word.**

The qualifications for the **seven men** are spelled out in verse 3. They were to be **men of honest report** ("men of good reputation," NASB, HCSB). They were to be **full of the Holy Ghost and wisdom.** Thus they were to be men who had the divine insight that comes when God's Spirit is in control of their lives. Were these the first deacons? Many people believe they were. The noun *deacon* is not used, but the verb from which it comes is found in verse 3, **serve** (*diakonein*). The names of the seven are given in verse 5. All had Greek names. This may not mean that they all were Greek-speaking disciples.

Several lessons can be learned from Acts 6:1-4, but this study focuses on taking timely action instead of doing nothing to resolve a potential problem.

Hearing and Doing (Jas. 1:22-25)

What is the proper way to hear the Word of God? Why must hearing lead to doing? What does the mirror analogy teach? What is the perfect law of liberty?

James 1:22-25: But be ye doers of the word, and not hearers only, deceiving your own selves. [23]For if any be a hearer of the word, and not a doer, he is like unto a man beholding his natural face in a glass: [24]for he beholdeth himself, and goeth his way, and straightway forgetteth what manner of man he was. [25]But whoso looketh into the perfect law of liberty, and continueth therein, he being not a forgetful hearer, but a doer of the work, this man shall be blessed in his deed.

James had just emphasized the importance of hearing the Word: "Let every man be swift to hear, slow to speak" (v. 19); "Receive with meekness the engrafted word, which is able to save your souls" (v. 21). Thus verses 22-25 do not minimize the value of hearing the Word, but they emphasize that true hearing leads to doing. James called his readers to be **doers of the word, and not hearers only.** This emphasis is found in the Old and the New Testaments. Both stress the value of hearing in the right way, but both measure the effectiveness of hearing by doing.

The Hebrews had such reverence for the Torah or Law that they felt that just hearing it was a blessing. Yet the Hebrew word for *hear* is the same word for *obey.* Jesus surely stressed the priority of *doing* as well as *hearing.* At the end of the Sermon on the Mount, He told the parable of the man who built his house on the rock and the man who built on the sand (Matt. 7:24-27). The difference between the two men was that the man with the rock foundation not only heard but also obeyed the word. The other man only heard the word but did not obey the word. James said that people who hear the word without doing the word deceive themselves. They are like the man whose house was built on the sand. They think they are secure, but they are only deceiving themselves.

James used an analogy to contrast only hearing with hearing and doing. He said that the former group are **like unto a man beholding his natural face in a glass** ("who looks at his face in a mirror," NIV): **for he beholdeth himself, and goeth his way, and straightway forgetteth what manner of man he was.** "The 'mirror' is key for understanding this section of James. In the ancient world the mirror, a specially shaped piece of polished metal, was used to inspect or decorate one's body. The ancient literature is replete with references to the mirror and its use as a metaphor for moral development."[1] Thus the mirror here probably stands for the moral and spiritual aspects of life. One who looks in a literal mirror sees only his face. One who looks into the mirror of the Word of God sees his moral and spiritual life. The problem is that such people forget what they saw and never act on what they beheld. This person is contrasted with the person who **looketh into the perfect law of liberty, and continueth therein.** This kind of person is **not a forgetful hearer, but a doer of the work.**

Some Bible students see another contrast in these verses—the intensity of the hearing. This view is based on the difference between the Greek words for **beholdeth** and **looketh.** The word in verse 24 is said to refer to only glancing at the mirror; the word in verse 25 is said to mean a careful look ("looks intently," NIV, HCSB).

There is a difference between the kinds of hearing, but it comes from the context more than from these two words. The key word in the wrong kind of hearing is **forgetteth**; the key word in the right kind of hearing is **continueth.** The wrong kind of hearers forget what they have heard; the right kind of hearers remember and continue to allow the word to direct their actions.

What is **the perfect law of liberty**? It seems to refer to the same thing as **the word.** James obviously was influenced by the teachings of Jesus. The gospel is not only gift but also demand. "The 'good news' of salvation brings with it an unavoidable, searching demand for complete obedience."[2]

How does this apply to you and me? First of all, it means that we must do everything possible to hear the Word of God. This involves personal reading and study. It includes studying with others. It emphasizes hearing the Word proclaimed. The Word of God is like a measuring stick for our lives. When we dare to expose ourselves to it, God is able to show us how we fail to meet His standards. If we truly have heard the Word, then we will live according to its teachings. This is one reason that we never graduate from Sunday School. During all our lives we need to see ourselves as God sees us and to make changes with His help.

Empty Religion and Genuine Religion (Jas. 1:26-27)

*What are some of the characteristics of empty religion? What are some of the characteristics of genuine religion? What are some of the sins of an unbridled tongue? What does it mean to visit orphans and widows? How does one stay **unspotted from the world**?*

James 1:26-27: **If any man among you seem to be religious, and bridleth not his tongue, but deceiveth his own heart, this man's religion is vain. 27Pure religion and undefiled before God and the Father is this, To visit the fatherless and widows in their affliction, and to keep himself unspotted from the world.**

James was dealing with basically the same issue throughout his letter. Sometimes he characterized it as the proper response to God's Word. In verses 26-27 he dealt with it in terms of empty and genuine religion. He dealt with three areas: speech, helping the needy, and living by God's standards not the world's.

Seem translates *dokei,* which has the idea of "thinks" (NASB, HCSB). James was addressing those who considered themselves to be religious. The person who thinks that he is religious **and bridleth not his tongue, but deceiveth his own heart, this man's religion is vain. Vain** means "worthless" (NIV, NASB, NRSV), "useless," (NKJV, HCSB), "empty." **Bridleth** is a word that literally refers to placing a bridle on an animal. Here and in 3:2-3 James used this analogy for an uncontrolled tongue. Some people see no relationship between how they talk each day and the religion they profess. The unbridled tongue can cause terrible damage. Even though people have trouble controlling their tongues, this verse shows that it is possible with God's help.

Pure religion and undefiled is lived out in the sight of **God and the Father.** That is, God recognizes our religion as genuine by what we do, not by what we claim for ourselves. **Visit** can mean "look after" (NIV, HCSB) or "care for" (NRSV). Two groups of needy people needed to be looked after: **the fatherless and widows.** People of genuine religion look after the needs of these groups **in their affliction.** This represents the aspect of genuine religion that involves caring for others rather than focusing on our own needs.

Finally, James named as another characteristic of genuine religion keeping ourselves **unspotted from the world.** When James wrote of **the world,** he was describing living and speaking by earthly standards. Worldly people are controlled by their evil desires, which result in strife among them. They either do not pray; or if they do, they pray purely selfish prayers (4:1-3). Friendship with the world is the opposite of friendship with God (v. 4). Believers are citizens of the eternal kingdom of God. Living by His standards is the opposite of living by the standards of the world.

Most of the people in our society claim some form of religion. Not all religions, even some of those that claim to be Christian, are genuine. Verses 26-27 list three characteristics of genuine religion versus empty religion: how we talk, how we serve, and how we live.

Claim and Evidence (Jas. 2:14-18)

What did James mean by **faith** *and* **works**? *Why do some people feel that James contradicted what Paul said about faith and works? What illustration did James use to show the difference between empty and genuine faith? Who is speaking in verse 18?*

James 2:14-18: What doth it profit, my brethren, though a man say he hath faith, and have not works? can faith save him? [15]If a brother or sister be naked, and destitute of daily food, [16]and one of you say unto them, Depart in peace, be ye warmed and filled; notwithstanding ye give them not those things which are needful to the body; what doth it profit? [17]Even so faith, if it hath not works, is dead, being alone. [18]Yea, a man may say, Thou hast faith, and I have works: show me thy faith without thy works, and I will show thee my faith by my works.

This is the most familiar and the most controversial passage in the Letter of James. It is known for its strong words about the necessity of both faith and works. James insisted that **faith, if it hath not works, is dead.** This is not different from his earlier contrasts between hearers only and hearers who are also doers and between empty religion and genuine religion. Apparently James was dealing with people whose religion was more of something they claimed to have than something real and transforming.

James asked two questions in verse 14: "What good is it, my brothers, if a man claims to have faith but has no deeds? Can such faith save him?" (NIV). The word for **faith** in the Greek of the second part of this verse has a definite article; thus, James was asking whether that kind of faith just described (the kind without works) could save anyone. He was not denying that faith does save. James was dealing with people who professed to believe in God but whose faith was only an intellectual belief. Notice verse 19: "Thou believest that there is one God; thou doest well: the devils also believe, and tremble." In other words, just believing in God's existence is not real faith. One evidence of this is that such faith does not produce good works.

Verses 15-16 give an example of a failure to practice good works. James pictured **a brother or sister** who was **naked, and destitute of daily food.** The word translated **naked** can also refer to someone who is poorly clothed, not totally naked. Even so, the picture is of someone in desperate need of the necessities of life. However, a fellow Christian sees this needy brother or sister and only says, **Depart in peace, be ye warmed and filled.** These words may have been intended as a pious sounding wish or as a prayer to God. If it was the latter, it was as if the person were saying, "May God provide you with clothes and food."

Words of comfort, encouragement, and prayer are important; however, words without actions do not reflect true faith. This is spelled out in the last part of verse 16. If all one person does for poorly clothed and hungry people is to wish them well or even to pray for them, this is not enough if the person is capable of meeting their needs but does nothing to help the needy ones. James' words in verses 15-16 are echoed in 1 John 3:17: "If anyone has material possessions and sees his brother in need but has no pity on him, how can the love of God be in him?" (NIV). John said that such indifference called in question the person's claim to have experienced the love of God. James said it called in question the person's claim to have faith in God.

Verse 18 isn't easy to understand, primarily because of the difficulty of telling who is speaking. The Greek manuscripts had no punctuation marks. Many Bible students and most translations assume that someone who held the view that James was attacking spoke the first part of the verse. Thus this part of the verse is often placed in quotation marks. "But someone will say, 'You have faith, and I have works'" (NKJV). The speaker took the position that faith and works were separable. Some had faith; others had works. James emphasized that they go together: "Show me your faith without your works, and I will show you my faith by my works" (NKJV). Or again, "Suppose someone disagrees and says, 'It is possible to have faith without doing kind deeds.' I would answer, 'Prove that you have faith without doing kind deeds, and I will prove that I have faith by doing them'" (CEV).

James' position is consistent with the rest of the Bible. The Bible teaches that we are saved by God's grace through faith, not by works added to faith. However, good works are the evidence of the reality of the faith (see Eph. 2:8-10). It's one thing to make a claim; it's another thing to produce the evidence.

❖ *Spiritual Transformations*

In this lesson we have seen four biblical contrasts that emphasize the necessity of transformed living by people of faith. Acts 6:1-4 shows that true believers take action to resolve problems. James 1:22-25 shows that those who truly hear the Word of God do what it says. James 1:26-27 shows that genuine religion controls the tongue, ministers to the needy, and lives by God's standards. James 2:14-18 shows that true faith is seen in the good works of one's life.

The impact of this lesson on your life should be to demonstrate your faith by right actions. This kind of genuine Christian living does at least four things: (1) It glorifies God: "Let your light so shine before men, that they may see your good works, and glorify your Father which is in heaven" (Matt. 5:16). (2) This kind of living provides the basis for a verbal testimony to the saving power of the Lord Jesus. (3) This kind of living assures us and others that we have been truly saved. (4) This kind of living is the only way to Christian peace and joy in the Lord.

As you evaluate your way of living with these passages and truths, in what areas do you need to walk closer to the Lord? _____

_____

What changes will you make to achieve this goal? _____

_____

Prayer of Commitment: Lord, forgive me for falling short of Your glory; help me to live for You each day.

---

[1]Kurt A. Richardson, "James," in *The New American Commentary*, vol. 36 [Nashville: Broadman & Holman Publishers, 1997], 95-96.

[2]Douglas J. Moo, *James*, in the Tyndale New Testament Commentaries [Grand Rapids: William B. Eerdmans Publishing Company, 1985], 84.

ENEMY TO ADVOCATE

Background Passage: Acts 8:1-3; 9:1-30
Focal Passage: Acts 9:1-16
Key Verse: Acts 9:15

❖ *Significance of the Lesson*

• The *Theme* of this lesson is Christ in you moves you from enemy to advocate.
• The *Life Question* this lesson seeks to challenge you with is, How has Jesus Christ changed my life?
• The *Biblical Truth* is that knowing Jesus as Savior and Lord changes a person from God's enemy to God's servant.
• The *Life Impact* is to help you continue to let Jesus transform your life.
• This is the **Evangelism Lesson** for this quarter.

Is Change Possible for Adults?

In the secular worldview, many are skeptical that adults can be changed from the patterns and habits of a lifetime. Others are more hopeful; they try to change for the better. New Year's resolutions, however, often fail to be kept. People want to be better, but they lack the will and power to do so.

In the Christian worldview, all are sinners who are unable to become what they should be in their own strength. Only the grace and power of God can transform people's lives. This transformation is made possible when people make Christ their Savior and Lord. He comes into a life and sets it on a new path, and the transformation also continues throughout life.

Conversion of the Apostle Paul

Next to Jesus Himself, Paul was most influential in shaping the Christian faith. The most important event in Paul's life was his experience of conversion when he met the Lord Jesus on the road to Damascus. The Book of Acts records three rather complete accounts of this experience. These three accounts testify to the importance of the conversion of Saul of Tarsus. In addition to this account in our Focal Passage, Paul spoke this same testimony to the Jerusalem mob that had tried to kill him (22:1-21) and to Herod Agrippa II (26:1-29). In addition, Paul often mentioned his conversion in his letters. Some significant passages include 1 Corinthians 15:8-10; Galatians 1:11-17,23-24; 2:7; Philippians 3:4-9; and 1 Timothy 1:12-16.

Names for Followers of Jesus in the Book of Acts

Three of the names for the followers of Jesus are found in the Focal Passage: **disciples,** those **of this way,** and **saints. Disciples** is used often in Acts. It is distinguished from the "apostles" (1:2,13,26). Disciples were learners and followers of Jesus. Those **of this way** ("the Way," NIV, HCSB, NRSV, NASB, NKJV) is used several times in Acts (16:17; 18:25-26; 19:9,23; 22:4; 24:14,22). It probably was influenced by Jesus' teachings about Himself as the Way and as the One who taught the way of life (Matt. 7:13-14; John 14:6). **Saints** appears in Acts for the first time in 9:13. It refers to those set apart by Christ and for Him. All disciples are saints. Other names include "believers" (5:14) "brethren" (11:1), and "Christians" (v. 26).

Word Study: *Chosen vessel*

In Acts 9:15 the Lord referred to Saul as **a chosen vessel** ("chosen instrument," NIV, HCSB, NASB). This expression combines the word for "vessel" (*skeuos*) with "chosen" (*ekloges*). *Skeuos* can refer to a jar or a pot (2 Tim. 2:20), or it can be used figuratively of a person (v. 21), as it is in our Focal Passage. Paul described Christians as vessels of clay in which is a precious treasure (2 Cor. 4:7). The latter word is closely related to the verb which means "to choose." Jesus said, "Ye have not chosen me, but I have chosen you" (John 15:16). It is also used here like the adjective "chosen," which often is translated "elect" (see Rom. 8:33). In Acts 9:15 **chosen vessel** applied to Saul in two ways. For one thing, the Lord had sought and chosen him; for another, he was to be an instrument through whom the Lord could work.

❖ *Search the Scriptures*

Saul of Tarsus led a vicious persecution of the early church in Jerusalem and went to Damascus to continue his work there. On the way he was blinded by a great light and heard a voice that proved to be the Lord Jesus. Saul was told that he had been persecuting the Lord. He was led blinded into Damascus. A believer named Ananias was sent to Saul, Saul's eyes were opened, and he was commissioned to be God's messenger to the Gentiles.

A Mission of Hate (Acts 9:1-2)

Why was Saul such a relentless persecutor of believers? What forms did Saul's persecution take? What were the goals of his persecution? What authority did he have for his trip to Damascus?

Verses 1-2: And Saul, yet breathing out threatenings and slaughter against the disciples of the Lord, went unto the high priest, ²and desired of him letters to Damascus to the synagogues, that if he found any of this way, whether they were men or women, he might bring them bound unto Jerusalem.

The first time Saul appears in the Bible story is at the death of Stephen. When Stephen was stoned to death, they "laid down their clothes at a young man's feet, whose name was Saul" (Acts 7:58). We also read: "And Saul was consenting unto his death" (8:1). Saul emerged as the leader of a terrible persecution of the believers in Jerusalem. Like some wild animal, "he made havoc of the church, entering into every house, and haling [hauling] men and women committed them to prison" (v. 3). Acts 8:4-40 shows how God brought good out of this evil by sending believers to many places preaching the good news.

Acts 9 begins where Acts 8:3 left off. **Saul** continued **breathing out threatenings and slaughter** ("murderous threats," NIV) **against the disciples of the Lord.** These were not idle threats, for Saul arrested and imprisoned both men and women. Later he said, "I persecuted this way [Way] unto the death" (22:4). And again, "When they were put to death, I gave my voice against them" (26:10). Saul pursued believers from house to house and from city to city. He relentlessly sought them out. He threatened them and made good his threats by imprisoning them (8:3; 9:2), beating them (22:19), seeking to make them blaspheme (26:11), and voting for their death (22:4; 26:10).

Saul was not content to confine his persecution to Jerusalem and Judea. He heard that there were disciples of Jesus in Damascus; and although it was six days' journey from Jerusalem, he **went unto the high priest.** Saul wanted **letters to Damascus to the synagogues** giving him authority to **bring** the followers of the Way **bound unto Jerusalem.** Damascus was not in the same government district as Jerusalem, but the high priest apparently had been given some authority over synagogues there. Saul could not rest until he had gone to Damascus to continue his persecution against followers of Jesus.

What was Saul seeking to accomplish? He later wrote that he wanted to destroy the church (Gal. 1:13) by doing everything possible to oppose the name of Jesus of Nazareth (Acts 26:9).

Why was Saul filled with such hatred for Jesus and His followers? He was a zealous Pharisee, and the Pharisees were opposing believers after the death of Stephen. The early believers offended the Sadducees by accusing the Sanhedrin of the death of Jesus. For a while, Pharisees such as Gamaliel were content to wait and see what happened (5:33-40); however, the preaching of Stephen aroused Pharisees such as Saul. Stephen attacked not only the veneration of the temple but also the rigid traditions of the Pharisees. His implication that Christ wanted a worldwide mission also disturbed the Pharisees.

Jesus had predicted that those who persecuted and killed His followers would think that they were serving God (John 16:2). That was surely true of Saul of Tarsus. He was a deeply religious man of great zeal for his religion. He considered persecution of Jesus' disciples to be a mark of his zeal (Phil. 3:6). The followers of Jesus seemed to threaten Saul's beliefs, and thus he sought to destroy them. In the process he said evil things against Jesus and His followers, and he did evil things to His followers (1 Tim. 1:13).

One of the clear lessons of verses 1-2 is the folly and evil of self-righteousness and pride. Saul was so self-righteous and proud that he did all these terrible things against the Lord and His people. In his book *Mere Christianity*, C. S. Lewis wrote a chapter on "The Great Sin." "There is one vice of which no man in the world is free; which every one in the world loathes when he sees it in someone else; and of which hardly any people, except Christians, ever imagine that they are guilty themselves. . . . The essential vice, the utmost evil, is Pride. . . . It was through Pride that the devil became the devil: Pride leads to every other vice: it is the complete anti-God state of mind."[1]

Saul was an enemy of Christ and the church. Paul the apostle wrote that all sinners are enemies of God, who need to be reconciled to God through Jesus Christ (Rom. 5:10; Col. 1:21). Some people are vocal opponents of God and the church. Many are not openly hostile, but they are separated from God by their sins—the most deceptive of which is self-righteousness.

An Encounter with Jesus (Acts 9:3-9)

When and where did Saul's encounter with the risen Lord take place? What did Saul see and hear? What did those with him see and hear? What did Jesus say first, and how did Saul respond? What did Jesus say second, and how did Saul respond? What did Jesus say third, and how did Saul respond?

Verses 3-9: And as he journeyed, he came near Damascus: and suddenly there shined round about him a light from heaven: ⁴and he fell to the earth, and heard a voice saying unto him, Saul, Saul, why persecutest thou me? ⁵And he said, Who art thou, Lord? And the Lord said, I am Jesus whom thou persecutest: it is hard for thee to kick against the pricks. ⁶And he trembling and astonished said, Lord, what wilt thou have me to do? And the Lord said unto him, Arise, and go into the city, and it shall be told thee what thou must do. ⁷And the men which journeyed with him stood speechless, hearing a voice, but seeing no man. ⁸And Saul arose from the earth; and when his eyes were opened, he saw no man: but they led him by the hand, and brought him into Damascus. ⁹And he was three days without sight, and neither did eat nor drink.

The events of these verses took place as Saul and his companions were **near Damascus.** It was about noon (22:6). **Suddenly there shined round about** Saul **a light from heaven** that was "above the brightness of the sun" (26:13). He and all who were with him fell to the earth (v. 14). Saul **heard a voice** that spoke words he understood. The others only heard a sound but did not understand any words (22:9).

Saul, Saul, why persecutest thou me? ("why are you persecuting Me?" NASB, NKJV, HCSB). Often in the Bible when a name was repeated it was repeated for emphasis (see 1 Sam. 3:10; Luke 10:41; 22:31). Saul realized that this voice from heaven was a divine voice; thus, he asked, **Who art thou, Lord?**

The answer must have been devastating for Saul. **I am Jesus whom thou persecutest.** Try to imagine what Saul felt when he heard that statement. He had said that Jesus was a fake, that He was not what He claimed, and that He had not been raised from the dead. Yet here was the risen Lord Jesus speaking to him. He had tried to destroy disciples of this One whom he had blasphemed. Now he realized that in persecuting the church, he had been attacking the Lord of glory. Every foundation of his past life was in ruins.

The words **it is hard for thee to kick against the pricks. And he trembling and astonished said, Lord, what wilt thou have me to do?** are not found in any Greek manuscript of the New Testament at 9:5 (hence the words are not found in the NIV, HCSB, NASB, or NRSV).

The words **it is hard for thee to kick against the pricks** ("goads," NKJV) are found at 26:14, however. A goad was a sharp stick or piece of metal used to keep oxen walking where they should. This was a common Greek and Roman proverb expressing the folly of resisting the will of the gods. Christians have interpreted the saying in two basic ways. Some Bible students believe that the words indicate that an inner struggle had been raging within the heart of Saul the persecutor. According to this view, although Saul outwardly seemed totally confident that he was right, some things were nagging at his conscience. Perhaps he was troubled by the way Stephen died and the way many disciples faced persecution. The other view is that only on the Damascus road did Saul realize that what he was doing was rebellion against the Lord. In either case, now he knew for sure.

Even though the words **Lord, what wilt thou have me to do?** are not in the Greek manuscripts of the New Testament, similar words are found in 22:10 as "Lord, what shall I do?" This was more than a question; it was a prayer. The Lord answered the prayer by telling Saul, **Arise, and go into the city, and it shall be told thee what thou must do.**

Later when Paul spoke of his encounter on the Damascus road, he spoke of it not as an inward vision but as hearing and seeing the Lord Jesus. Paul always spoke of seeing the risen Lord. Ananias spoke of the Lord who appeared to Saul on the road (9:17). Paul saw the Lord in the glory of the light (22:11). And he listed himself as one of those who saw the risen Lord (1 Cor. 15:8).

The immediate physical effect of this encounter with Jesus left Saul unable to see. His traveling companions knew that something unique had happened. They were **speechless** during the time of the light and the sound, which Saul heard as the voice of Jesus. After the light was gone, they discovered that Saul could not see. Therefore, **they led him**

by the hand, and brought him into Damascus. How different was this entry from the way Saul had planned! He had pictured himself as entering the city as a powerful man. Instead, he was led in as a blind man, dependent on others.

After arriving, **he was three days without sight, and neither did eat nor drink.** The proud persecutor was now a blind man. He fasted for three days. Verses 11-12 show that the Lord spoke to him during that time, and that Saul not only fasted but also prayed.

Was Saul's encounter intended to be a model for all conversions? The answer is no and yes. It is not a model in the sense of the circumstances nor even in the dramatic way it happened. There was only one Saul of Tarsus, and only one Damascus road encounter of the Lord with him. However, coming to know Christ involves some kind of personal encounter with Him. He still steps across the pathways of our lives and calls us to repent of our sins and to follow Him as Savior and Lord. Sometimes this encounter is emotionally charged, like a violent storm; in other cases the encounter is peaceful, like a calm breeze. Emotions and circumstances involved in individual conversions differ, but following Jesus involves personal faith. No one drifts into the kingdom of God; each enters by responding to the Lord in his or her own way.

I. Howard Marshall wrote, "Those elements of what happened to Saul near Damascus do not usually happen to people nowadays. But—and this is crucial—the conversion to a total commitment to Jesus and living for Him is essential. Many people are not living lives totally opposed to Jesus; those people may be respectable and well-intentioned, and perhaps (like me) brought up as 'Christian' from their birth. But—and again this is crucial—they still need to make a full commitment of themselves to Jesus."[2]

A Radical Transformation (Acts 9:10-16)

Who was Ananias? How did he help Saul? How did the Lord reveal His grace to Saul? How did Saul respond to the divine revelation? What factors show the spiritual transformation in Saul's life?

Verses 10-16: **And there was a certain disciple at Damascus, named Ananias; and to him said the Lord in a vision, Ananias. And he said, Behold, I am here, Lord.** [11]**And the Lord said unto him, Arise, and go into the street which is called Straight, and inquire in the house of Judas for one called Saul, of Tarsus: for, behold, he** prayeth, [12]and hath seen in a vision a man named Ananias coming in, and putting his hand on him, that he might receive his sight. [13]Then Ananias answered, Lord, I have heard by many of this man, how much evil he hath done to thy saints at Jerusalem: [14]and here he hath authority from the chief priests to bind all that call on thy name. [15]But the Lord said unto him, Go thy way: for he is a chosen vessel unto me, to bear my name before the Gentiles, and kings, and the children of Israel: [16]for I will show him how great things he must suffer for my name's sake.

Ananias was **a certain disciple at Damascus.** When Paul defended himself before the mob in Jerusalem, he said that Ananias was "a devout man according to the law, having a good report of all the Jews which dwelt there" (22:12). When **the Lord in a vision** called his name, Ananias (like the young Samuel in the Old Testament) said, **Behold, I am here, Lord.** Then the Lord told him to go to where **Saul, of Tarsus,** waited. The Lord told him where to find Saul. Ananias knew what had happened in Jerusalem. Therefore, he told the Lord that he had **heard . . . how much evil** Saul had **done to** the Lord's **saints at Jerusalem.** Ananias also knew that Saul had come to Damascus **to bind all that call on** the Lord's **name.** But the Lord still told Ananias to **go** to Saul. The Lord told Ananias that He had given Saul **a vision** of **a man named Ananias coming** to open his eyes. The Lord also told Ananias that Saul was praying.

What Ananias did to help Saul is found in verses 17-18 and in 22: 13-16. Ananias went to where Saul was. Saul's heart must have leaped when he heard that Ananias had come. Ananias called Saul "brother." This act of love and courage by Ananias was reassuring to the blind former persecutor. One whom he had come to arrest called him a brother! Ananias was used to open Saul's blinded eyes. Paul may have had this in mind when he later wrote, "God, who commanded the light to shine out of the darkness, hath shined in our hearts, to give the light of the knowledge of the glory of God in the face of Jesus Christ" (2 Cor. 4:6). Ananias then baptized Saul and assured him of the cleansing of his sins (22:16). He also delivered to Saul the Lord's commission to serve Him.

How did the Lord reveal His grace to Saul? First of all, the Lord did not strike him down to hell when He confronted him on the Damascus road. He accused him of persecuting the Lord and His people, and He blinded his eyes; however, He did not punish Saul as he deserved. This was a sign of the Lord's grace. Second, the Lord sent Ananias to him to do the things mentioned in the previous paragraph. Paul's doctrine of justification by faith grew out of his experience. He was guilty and deserved eternal condemnation. Yet the Lord was willing to accept him although he was unacceptable.

How did Paul respond to the divine revelation? When he was on the Damascus road, he prayed asking the Lord what he was to do. While he waited three days, he prayed. When Ananias told him to be baptized, he was baptized. He began to preach that Jesus is the Son of God, causing the people to be astonished that the persecutor was now a witness for Jesus (9:17-22).

The commission of Saul is found in verses 15-16. It focuses on three factors in Saul's new life. For one thing, Saul was **a chosen vessel** unto the Lord, who had chosen him and now called him to fulfill the divine purpose for his life. Saul's energies were to be redirected for the cause of the Lord rather than against Him. Second, his mission was to **bear** the Lord's **name before the Gentiles, and kings, and the children of Israel.** Saul's mission to the Gentiles later emerged as his primary mission (22:21). Third, he was to learn **how great things he must suffer for** the Lord's **name's sake.** "The one who once was the church's most vehement persecutor would now be the one who would willingly accept persecution for the sake of the name. . . . In nothing is his conversion more clearly illustrated than in his transformation from persecutor to persecuted."[3]

Paul continually was amazed and grateful about two aspects of the grace of the Lord toward him. For one thing, he was thrilled and motivated by the forgiveness of his great sins; second, he was thankful that the Lord had entrusted to such a sinner the mission of serving Him by telling others of God's love. He wrote: "I thank Christ Jesus our Lord, who has given me strength, that he considered me faithful, appointing me to his service. Even though I was once a blasphemer and a persecutor and a violent man, I was shown mercy because I acted in ignorance and unbelief. The grace of our Lord was poured out on me abundantly, along with the faith and love that are in Christ Jesus. Here is a trustworthy saying that deserves full acceptance: Christ Jesus came into the world to save sinners—of whom I am the worst" (1 Tim. 1:12-15, NIV).

Charles Colson was converted on August 12, 1973. His conversion became one of the most highly publicized of the 20th century. Colson had been Special Counsel for President Nixon and was known as the president's "hatchet man." Unlike Saul, Colson was a purely secular man. He had never heard the word *evangelical.* Some Christians in

Washington involved him in their prayer group. He became convicted of his sin and was converted. Since this was during the Watergate crisis, news of Colson's conversion was heard with skeptical ears.

However, in the years since then, the reality of Colson's conversion is obvious in the transformation of his life. Reflecting on his conversion after several years of being a Christian, Colson listed questions he often is asked. One is "How do you see yourself—that ambitious, hard-driving perfectionist—as having changed in the years since your conversion?" He wrote, "God doesn't give you a whole set of new gifts when He converts you. Paul the zealous persecutor became Paul the zealous propagator of the faith. We're all like that. God simply redirects our gifts and priorities. My priorities before were power, wealth, fame; today I believe they're knowing and loving God, my relationships with my family, which have become *much* more meaningful to me, and my desire to serve the Lord."[4]

❖ Spiritual Transformations

Saul of Tarsus was a self-righteous, violent persecutor of the church. The Lord confronted him on the road to Damascus and revealed Himself to Saul. The Lord sent Ananias to call Saul to the new life that the Lord had for him. Saul the persecutor was a hard-driving zealous person who opposed Jesus; Paul the missionary would be a hard-driving zealous person who preached Jesus.

One sure sign of genuine conversion is not so much the emotional intensity of the initial encounter as the continuing reality of our walk with the Lord and the continuing transformation into His likeness and image.

*Have you ever accepted Jesus Christ as your Lord and Savior?*____
*What happened when you were converted?*_____
What changes has Christ made in your life? _____

Prayer of Commitment: Lord, continue Your work of grace in me and make me what You want me to be.

[1]C. S. Lewis, *Mere Christianity* [New York: The Macmillan Company, 1958], 94.

[2]I. Howard Marshall, "The Apostle Paul—A Life Changed by Grace," *Decision Magazine*, January 2001, 32.

[3]John B. Polhill, "Acts," in *The New American Commentary*, vol. 26 [Nashville: Broadman Press, 1992], 237.

[4]Charles Colson, *Who Speaks for God?* [Westchester, IL: Crossway Books, 1985], 177,179-180.

DEVALUED TO VALUED

Background Passage: Exodus 1:1–2:10; Hebrews 11:23
Focal Passage: Exodus 1:15-17,20-22; 2:1-10; Hebrews 11:23
Key Verse: Hebrews 11:23

❖ *Significance of the Lesson*

• The *Theme* of this lesson is that Christ in you causes you to affirm the value of all human life.
• The *Life Question* this lesson challenges us with is, Do I care enough to seek to protect human life?
• The *Biblical Theme* is that human life is to be valued and protected.
• The *Life Impact* is to help you value and protect human life.
• This is the annual **Sanctity of Human Life Lesson.**

Worldviews About Human Life

In the secular worldview, human life is cheap. Human beings are disposable. Television, movies, video games, and music glorify violence and death. Society is so saturated with violence and brutality that people become desensitized to killing. The outcome of devaluing human life is a culture steeped in death—a culture in which abortion, the selling of fetal body parts, and assisted suicide are acceptable, and in which children kill children.

In the biblical worldview, human life is precious. Every human life is created by God in His image and has inestimable value. All human beings, including unborn children, are to be treated with dignity and respect and are to be protected.

Sanctity of Human Life Sunday

The third Sunday of January is the Sunday set aside to emphasize the sanctity of human life. This particular lesson focuses on abortion. The Bible does not deal explicitly with abortion, but it has many teachings and stories that apply to the issue. The Focal Passages deal with the slaughter of the boy babies of the Hebrews by order of Pharaoh. They were killed after they were born, but the principles also apply in many cases to children before they are born.

Word Study: *Feared God*

The Hebrew word for **fear** is used over and over in the Old Testament. On the one hand, people are told to fear God, and if they do, not to fear anything else (see, for example, Num. 14:9). The midwives acted as they did because they **feared God.** Thus fear of God is not cringing fear that paralyzes action; it is a life of reverence for God that leads to trust, obedience, and bold action.

❖ *Search the Scriptures*

Exodus 1:1–2:10 tells how the Hebrews became slaves in Egypt, how God preserved them from Pharaoh's plan to destroy them, and how a deliverer was sent in Moses. When Pharaoh ordered the midwives to kill the boy babies of the Hebrews immediately after birth, the midwives refused because they feared God. When Pharaoh ordered all people to throw boy babies into the Nile, a child—conceived and born to a couple from the tribe of Levi—was set afloat in the Nile River. When Pharaoh's daughter found him, Moses' sister Miriam, with the permission of the princess, arranged for the child's care. The child thus delivered was Moses, and the one chosen to be his nurse was his mother!

Be Courageous (Ex. 1:15-17,20-21)

Who was the king of Egypt, what was his policy, and why did he command the action he did? Who were the midwives, what did they do, why did they do it, and what was their worldview? What principles from these verses relate to abortion? These questions are addressed in comments on these verses.

Exodus 1:15-17,20-21: **And the king of Egypt spake to the Hebrew midwives, of which the name of the one was Shiphrah, and the name of the other Puah: [16]And he said, When ye do the office of a midwife to the Hebrew women, and see them upon the stools; if it be a son, then ye shall kill him: but if it be a daughter, then she** shall live. [17]But the midwives feared God, and did not as the king of Egypt commanded them, but saved the men children alive.

. . . .

[20]Therefore God dealt well with the midwives: and the people multiplied, and waxed very mighty. [21]And it came to pass, because the midwives feared God, that he made them houses.

The king of Egypt is another name for **Pharaoh** (1:19,22), a title for all kings of ancient Egypt. Three Pharaoh's are mentioned in the closing chapters of Genesis and in the Book of Exodus. The first was the Pharaoh under whom Joseph rose to power and under whom the Hebrews settled in Egypt (see Gen. 39–47). The Pharaoh in Exodus 1:8–2:23a is called the Pharaoh of the oppression. His successor is called the Pharaoh of the deliverance (2:23b–14:31). The Pharaoh of the deliverance was the one whom Moses challenged to let the Israelites leave Egypt.

The Pharaoh of the oppression was the new king who arose "who knew not Joseph" (1:8). He did not immediately succeed the Pharaoh who knew Joseph personally. A number of generations intervened between Exodus 1:5 when 70 of Jacob's family moved to Egypt and the oppression. Exodus 12:40-41 says that the Hebrews were in Egypt 430 years. By the time of the oppression, the number of Hebrews had become so great that Pharaoh considered them a threat. He "knew not Joseph" in the sense that he totally disagreed with the policy of allowing the Hebrews to continue to grow and multiply. He considered them a threat, and thus made them into slaves (1:9-14). He apparently intended to work them to death. However, the Hebrews continued to multiply.

Thus Pharaoh had to come up with a second plan to destroy them. He ordered the **Hebrew midwives** to **kill** the boy babies as soon as they were born; girls were to be spared. **Stools** were the "birthstools" (NKJV) or "the delivery stool" (NIV).

Although this practice of infanticide was not abortion in the strict sense of the word, it is very close to what is done in selective abortion and in partial-birth abortions. The grim reality of partial-birth abortion—which can be performed on a full-term pre-born baby—is as follows: "A partial birth abortion is performed on pre-born babies usually beginning at the fifth month of development, and takes three days to complete. The abortionist begins by dilating the woman's cervix for two days. Then, on the third day, he uses forceps to deliver the entire baby, except for the head. At this stage of development, the baby's head is too large to fit through the woman's cervix, so the abortionist uses blunt surgical scissors to stab the baby at the base of the skull. He then inserts a vacuum tube and sucks the child's brain out so he can collapse the skull and pull the dead baby through the cervical opening."[1]

We are not told how the midwives were expected to kill the babies, but any method would be violent, as Paul Fowler pointed out concerning our contemporary methods. "The methods of abortion are physically violent. Whether it be a sharp, double-edged curette (or knife) by which the child is unceremoniously dissected, or the suction of the inserted tube which tears apart the tiny child, or the burning effect of the injected saline solution on the tender skin of the child while simultaneously poisoning the baby internally—there is no term more appropriate for such cruel methods than *violence*."[2]

What would Pharaoh have done if he had the tools of modern technology that enable a baby's sex to be determined before birth? Would he have availed himself of this technology to order the abortion of all male babies—as is done in some places in the world today with female babies? We can only imagine! Many people today assume that anything that technology makes possible ought to be used. The questions of right and wrong are not asked; instead, the assumption is, "If we can do it, do it."

The names of **the Hebrew midwives** were **Shiphrah** and **Puah.** Only two names are mentioned, but these two were probably the heads of or the names of larger groups of midwives. The number of Hebrews was so great that only two individuals likely could not deliver all the babies. These two "were no doubt the heads of the whole profession, and were expected to communicate their instructions to their associates."[3]

The orders of the king were clear, **but the midwives feared God** more than they feared the king. Therefore, they **did not as the king of Egypt commanded them, but saved the men children alive** ("let the boys live," NIV). When the king realized that his orders were being disobeyed, he called for the midwives to explain their failure to obey him (v. 18). The midwives gave as their reason the fact that the Hebrew women gave birth so quickly that the midwives were unable to arrive before the birth (v. 19). This answer was obviously an evasion, but this is further proof that the order was to kill the boy babies as soon as they were born.

Why did the midwives disobey the king of Egypt? Keep in mind that this was a risky thing to do. The only explanation given in the Bible is that they **feared God.** What does this explanation and their actions reveal about their worldview? The most obvious thing is that they placed God and His will at the center of their lives and actions. They were so committed to God that they took risks for Him. What did sparing the boy babies have to with their fear of God? Their reverence for God led to their reverence for human life. By the same token, "their reverence for life reflected a reverence for God."[4]

From their actions we may surmise that the midwives believed human life is precious because human beings are made in God's image (Gen. 1:27). Thus they knew that it was a sin against God to take a human life (9:5-6). They also believed that people who follow the Lord must act for good in obedience to His will. They took great risks because they feared God more than they feared Pharaoh. Thus we read in verse 21 that **because the midwives feared God . . . he made them houses. Made them houses** means that God established "house-holds" (NKJV, NASB) for them. Putting it in a clearer way, God "gave them families of their own" (NIV; similarly, the NRSV).

Both the Old and New Testaments make clear that God's people are not only not to exploit the weak and helpless but that they also are to help them, including defending them against those who threaten them. No group is so helpless as unborn babies. Those who defend them are acting according to this basic biblical principle.

Act in Faith (Ex. 1:22–2:4; Heb. 11:23)

*What was Pharaoh's third attempt to limit the growth of the Hebrews? What do all Pharaoh's acts reveal about his worldview? What is implied about when life begins by the words **conceived, and bare a son**? What did the parents of Moses do? Why did they do this? What was their worldview?*

Exodus 1:22: And Pharaoh charged all his people, saying, Every son that is born ye shall cast into the river, and every daughter ye shall save alive.

Pharaoh's third attempt to destroy the Hebrews was his order for all people to throw any Hebrew boy baby into the Nile. He apparently had given up on the midwives. Now he ordered **all his people,** that is, the Egyptians, to obey his order. **Every son that is born** refers to the same group mentioned in 1:16. Each Hebrew boy baby was to be **cast into the river.** This was a less messy way of killing the babies, but theoretically just as effective—assuming that his people obeyed his order. We have no record of how many Egyptians did what their king ordered. We know that his own daughter defied him.

In light of the three attempts of Pharaoh to destroy the Hebrews, what does this indicate about his worldview? We know from Egyptian history that the Pharaoh was considered to be a god. If one thinks he is a god, then he can do as he pleases. Pharaoh practiced a form of genocide against an entire ethnic group in his land. He considered them a threat. Very likely he considered them as of far less value than the Egyptians. He treated the Hebrews as if they were less than human. Pharaoh had no respect for human life—at least not for the Hebrews. He was willing to do anything to achieve his will and to destroy them.

His worldview was similar to the Nazi attitude toward the Jews. Most attempts at genocide use names designed to hide the hideous nature of what they are doing. The Nazi name for the systematic elimination of Jews was "the final solution." More recently, some of the Serbs used the term "ethnic cleansing" to describe their practice of genocide. The word *euthanasia* means literally "good death." Abortion terms often cloak what it really is. Proponents of abortion refer to the "termination of pregnancy" or "removal of fetal tissue." The practice of killing some of the fetuses in a multiple pregnancy is known as "selective reduction." In Canada, the late-term abortion of fetuses with genetic abnormalities, including Down's Syndrome, is called "genetic termination."

Exodus 2:1-4: And there went a man of the house of Levi, and took to wife a daughter of Levi. ²And the woman conceived, and bare a son: and when she saw him that he was a goodly child, she hid him three months. ³And when she could not longer hide him, she took for him an ark of bulrushes, and daubed it with slime and with pitch, and put the child therein; and she laid it in the flags by the river's brink. ⁴And his sister stood afar off, to wit what would be done to him.

. . . .

Hebrews 11:23: By faith Moses, when he was born, was hid three months of his parents, because they saw he was a proper child; and they were not afraid of the king's commandment.

The mother of Moses **conceived, and bare a son.** "Some forty times Scripture refers to conception as the start of new life in the womb of the mother. In the Genesis narratives alone, the phrase 'conceived and bore' is found eleven times. The close pairing of the two words clearly emphasizes conception, not birth, as the starting point of life."[5]

Most people today recognize that life begins at conception, but some distinguish between human life and a human person. Modern technology has shown clearly that the baby is alive and develops quickly within the womb. However, the proponents of abortion say that only at some later point does the living being become a person. Many place this at birth; others place it at some point of development within the womb. The Bible sees the new life as a person from the beginning—one created in the image of God. When David's infant son died, he said, "I will go to him, but he will not return to me" (2 Sam. 12:23, NIV). When Elizabeth first saw Mary after the miraculous conception of Jesus, "the babe leaped in her womb" (Luke 1:41). Jacob and Esau struggled together within Rebekah's womb (Gen. 25:22). In addition, there are a number of verses that refer to the work of God in forming the baby within the womb (see Ps. 139:13-16; Jer. 1:4-5; Job 31:15). James Dobson wrote: "The Bible does not address itself directly to the practice of abortions. However, I was amazed to observe how many references are made in both the Old and New Testaments to God's personal acquaintance with children *prior* to birth. Not only is He aware of their gestations but He is specifically knowledgeable of them as unique individuals and personalities."[6]

One strong reason for believing that this is a correct understanding of the Scripture is the opposition of early Christians to abortion and to all forms of infanticide. "A first-century catechism placed those who are 'killers of the child, who abort the mold [image] of God,' between murderers and adulterers, all embarked on 'the Way of Darkness.'"[7] In their book *Whatever Happened to the Human Race?* Francis A. Schaeffer and C. Everett Koop stressed that from the earliest times until modern times the church opposed abortion. They quoted from Tertullian, one of the early church fathers, "For us murder is once for all forbidden; so even the child in the womb, while yet the mother's blood is still being drawn on to form the human being, it is not lawful for us to destroy. To forbid birth is only quicker murder. It makes no difference whether one take away the life once born or destroy it as it comes to birth. He is a man, who is to be a man; the fruit is always present in the seed." They further pointed out that a different humanistic worldview has spawned the modern toleration of this practice and other acts that devalue human life.[8]

Moses' parents (Amram and Jochebed [JAHK-uh-bed], 6:20) were not willing to have their son killed. Therefore, Jochebed **hid him** for

three months. When she could not longer hide him, she acted to save his life in another way. **She took for him an ark of bulrushes** ("got a papyrus basket for him," NIV, NRSV) and made it so that it was water-tight. Then she put her son in the basket and **laid it in the flags** ("reeds," NIV) **by the river's brink** ("bank," NIV). She did not just set the ark adrift aimlessly. It was carefully placed, as verses 5-10 confirm. Moses' sister Miriam was stationed so she could observe what happened.

Why did Moses' parents act as they did? Hebrews 11:23 says that they exercised **faith** in doing this. They believed it was God's will that their child be spared. They believed that children are a gift and trust from God (see Ps. 127). They did all they could, and they trusted God to do the rest.

They also acted in love for their baby. After all, this was their child, and they loved him. They already had two children (Miriam and Aaron), and those were difficult days for raising a child. But they had no intention of failing to do all they could to save him. How differently they acted from those who use abortion as a means of birth control—especially those who cite their economic conditions as justification!

The reasons given for ending a child's life before birth are many and varied. Most of the excuses do not have to do with unhealthy babies but simply with not wanting a child. The Bible teaches that little children are especially precious to the Heavenly Father. Jesus used strong words to warn against sinning against little ones (Matt. 18:6). He taught that little ones are special to God (v. 10).

Do What You Can (Ex. 2:5-10)

Did Moses' mother place the ark where Pharaoh's daughter would find it? Was Miriam's speech rehearsed? Why did Pharaoh's daughter rescue Moses, a Hebrew child whom her father had ordered to be killed? Why did the child need a nurse? Did Pharaoh's daughter know that the nurse was Moses' mother? What difference to later history would have resulted if Moses had been killed as an infant? What lessons about abortion are found in these verses?

Exodus 2:5-10: And the daughter of Pharaoh came down to wash herself at the river; and her maidens walked along by the river's side; and when she saw the ark among the flags, she sent her maid to fetch it. ⁶And when she had opened it, she saw the child: and, behold, the babe wept. And she had compassion on him, and said,

This is one of the Hebrews' children. [7]Then said his sister to Pharaoh's daughter, Shall I go and call to thee a nurse of the Hebrew women, that she may nurse the child for thee? [8]And Pharaoh's daughter said to her, Go. And the maid went and called the child's mother. [9]And Pharaoh's daughter said unto her, Take this child away, and nurse it for me, and I will give thee thy wages. And the woman took the child, and nursed it. [10]And the child grew, and she brought him unto Pharaoh's daughter, and he became her son. And she called his name Moses: and she said, Because I drew him out of the water.

When Moses' mother placed him in the basket and left him among the reeds, did she place him where she felt that Pharaoh's daughter would find and save him? Some Bible students believe she did; others disagree. The Bible does not tell us whether she knew he was near the place where Pharaoh's daughter came to bathe.

We know that Miriam was stationed nearby, but we are not told whether her speech was rehearsed. It may have been if Jochebed expected the princess to find the infant. However, if she did not have this expectation, Miriam's speech was the result of God's giving the girl wisdom and courage to make her suggestion.

One thing is sure: Moses' family did all they could to try to save the life of the infant. At the same time, they trusted God to do what only He could do. There is no contradiction between God's providence and human actions. It takes both.

One of the interesting things in this story is the prominent role of women. The midwives spared the boy babies they were ordered to kill. Moses' mother hid him and then did what she could to protect him. Miriam spoke up to suggest that her mother be named the nurse for the baby. Pharaoh's daughter saved him, enlisted a nurse during his young years, and raised him as her son.

We do not know the name of Pharaoh's daughter, nor do we know whether she had children of her own. She found the basket and the baby, and when she saw the baby crying, **she had compassion on him.** Immediately she realized that this was **one of the Hebrews' children.** She no doubt knew of her father's order. What other reason would there be for a baby to be hidden in a basket at the river?

Why did she spare the child? One word explains why—**compassion.** She saw this helpless living child, and her heart was touched by his plight. As she was pondering her discovery, Moses' sister boldly asked if the princess wanted her to find **a nurse of the Hebrew women, that**

she may nurse the child. Did the princess recognize that this was part of a plan? If so, did she know that the **nurse** was the mother of the child? The Bible does not tell us. We do know that she recognized a need for a nurse. The word **nurse** refers to a wet nurse. The baby was probably crying because of hunger. The princess agreed to let Miriam find a nurse, and in this way God's providence placed the precious child back in the care of his own mother until he was weaned. Look at the picture in verse 9: Jochebed **took the child, and nursed it.** We can see in our imaginations the joy and relief on the face of Moses' mother as she held her own son and nursed him. His life had been spared.

After the child was weaned, Moses' mother **brought him unto Pharaoh's daughter, and he became her son.** We are not told what Pharaoh's daughter said to her father about her deliverance and adoption of a Hebrew child. At any rate, he obviously did not forbid her actions. He probably did not feel that one child posed any threat to him and to Egypt. He may even have become fond of his adopted grandson. Whatever was the attitude of Pharaoh, the attitude of his daughter is clear. When she looked at the baby in the basket, she did not see an enemy to be destroyed but a child to be rescued. As Moses grew up, she looked on her adopted son as her own.

Moses' mother had looked for some alternative to allowing her son to be killed. She faced a dilemma similar to girls and woman who are in a situation in which they are pressured to have an abortion. She was led by God to find an option. This is one of the functions of crisis pregnancy centers. They help women recognize their options. Adoption is one of these options.

Pharaoh's daughter **called his name Moses.** The name **Moses** (*Mosheh*) has a double meaning. On the one hand, it is similar to a Hebrew word meaning "to draw out" (*mashah*; **because I drew him out of the water**). On the other hand, it is a form of an old Egyptian verb meaning "(such and such a god) is born" (as in the Egyptian names Ahmose and Thutmose).

The later life of this rescued baby was powerful in its impact. What a difference if Moses had been killed as an infant! We cannot help but speculate what impact would have been made if each of the millions of aborted lives had been allowed to live and make their contributions.

What a waste is the loss of such individuals! The World Health Organization estimates that *each day* between 100,000 and 150,000 induced abortions occur and about 36 to 53 million worldwide each year!

Further, abortions kill about 70,000 woman annually and account for about 13 percent of all maternal deaths.[9] The number of abortions in the United States between 1973 and 1998 is estimated at 38 million.[10]

❖ Spiritual Transformations

Because Pharaoh felt that the Hebrews were a threat to his well-being, he ordered the midwives to kill the boy babies immediately after birth. This is very much like partial-birth abortions.

Because the midwives feared God, they valued human life and refused to kill the babies.

The linking of conception with birth is one of many ways the Bible shows that God is involved from the beginning and that human life begins with conception.

Because she loved her child and had faith in God, Jochebed sought ways to save the life of her infant son.

Because she had compassion on the Hebrew baby, Pharaoh's daughter secured a Hebrew nurse and raised the child as her own.

Because the life of the infant Moses was spared, he was able to make his impact on history.

Do you value the unborn? Why or why not? _____

_____

How do you or might you protect them? _____

_____

Prayer of Commitment: Lord, help me to value and protect the unborn.

[1]From the Library of Concerned Women for America at www.cwfa.org, revised Sept. 27, 1999.

[2]Paul B. Fowler, *Abortion: Toward an Evangelical Consensus* [Portland: Multnomah Press, 1987], 192.

[3]C. F. Keil, "The Pentateuch," vol. 3, in *Commentary on the Old Testament*, vol. I [Grand Rapids: William B. Eerdmans Publishing Company, 1983 reprint], 424.

[4]Walter C. Kaiser, Jr., "Exodus," in vol. 2 of *The Expositor's Bible Commentary* [Grand Rapids: Zondervan Publishing House, 1990], 306.

[5]Fowler, *Abortion*, 136.

[6]James Dobson and Gary Bergel, *The Decision of Life* [Colorado Springs: Focus on the Family, 1993], 8.

[7]Fowler, *Abortion*, 17.

[8]Francis A. Schaeffer and C. Everett Koop, *Whatever Happened to the Human Race?* [Old Tappan, NJ: Fleming H. Revell Company, 1979], 85.

[9]From *The Journal of the American Medical Association*, September 22/29, 1999.

[10]Statistics from The National Right to Life Committee at www.NRLC.org/abortion.

USELESS TO USEFUL

Background Passage: Philemon 1-25
Focal Passage: Philemon 8-21
Key Verse: Philemon 11

❖ *Significance of the Lesson*

• The *Theme* of this lesson is that Christ in you moves you to see people's usefulness in the kingdom of God.

• The *Life Question* this lesson seeks to address is, Why do I think some people are useless?

• The *Biblical Truth* is that all believers can be useful in the kingdom of God.

• The *Life Impact* is to help you see and affirm others' usefulness in the kingdom of God.

Useless or Useful?

In the secular worldview, some people are looked down on as useless. You've heard the expressions before: "You'll never amount to anything." "You don't have what it takes." "You're not worth my time and effort." "You're a hopeless case." Some people say such things to children, youth, spouses, parents, friends, employees, lost people, and Christians who have failed. When mistakes are made, these are never forgiven or forgotten. Only a person's worst experiences are used to judge him or her. Even in the church some people make others feel they are useless.

In the biblical worldview, God's transforming grace is available to all. God sees us not as we are or as we have been, but He sees us as we can become. By His grace any person can become useful in the kingdom of God. Such transformation is experienced through one's relationship with God through Christ. Christians are God's instruments in helping lost people find Christ and realize their potential usefulness.

Slavery in the First Century

Slavery was a deeply ingrained social and economic reality in first-century Greek and Roman life. In most major cities slaves out-numbered free people. Although some masters treated their slaves with consideration, others treated them harshly. In either case, the masters usually were allowed to treat their slaves as nothing more than property to do with as they chose. Masters lived in fear of slave up-risings. They severely punished slaves who tried to run away. Some of the early Christians were slaves, such as Onesimus [oh-NESS-ih-muhs]. Only a few like Philemon [figh-LEE-muhn] were wealthy enough to own slaves. The writers of the New Testament did not call on slaves to rebel against their masters but rather to submit themselves to their masters. Christianity was in no position to oppose such a deeply entrenched system, but the New Testament sowed seeds that even-tually contributed to the end of slavery in Christian nations.

Word Study: *Unprofitable, Profitable, Onesimus*

The name **Onesimus** occurs as a common adjective meaning "profitable" or "useful." This adjective is from the verb *oninemi*, which means "to bring profit or value to someone" (see Philem. 20). Paul reinforced his point in verse 11 by using a synonym and an antonym from another root: *achreston* means "unprofitable" and *euchreston* means "profitable."

❖ *Search the Scriptures*

Paul wrote Philemon telling him that Onesimus—Philemon's runaway slave who had become a believer—who had been unprofitable to Philemon was now profitable. He spoke of the value of Onesimus as a brother in Christ. Paul asked Philemon to welcome back Onesimus, whom Paul was sending home.

Useful (Philem. 8-11)

*Who were Philemon and Onesimus? On what basis did Paul make his appeal to Philemon? In what two ways did Paul describe himself? Why did Paul refer to Onesimus as his **son**? In what way was Onesimus* *unprofitable* to Philemon? In what way could he be *profitable*? These questions are addressed in comments on these verses.

Verses 8-11: Wherefore, though I might be much bold in Christ to enjoin thee that which is convenient, ⁹yet for love's sake I rather beseech thee, being such an one as Paul the aged, and now also a prisoner of Jesus Christ. ¹⁰I beseech thee for my son Onesimus, whom I have begotten in my bonds: ¹¹which in time past was to thee unprofitable, but now profitable to thee and to me.

The Letter to Philemon is Paul's shortest letter and his most personal New Testament letter. Behind it lies an intriguing story, which can be pieced together from reading the letter and in some cases from reading between the lines. Some facts are clear, but other parts of the story are educated guesses. Based on verses 1-2, Paul, who was a prisoner at the time, wrote to Philemon, a fellow Christian and beloved friend of Paul. The apostle also included in his greeting Apphia [AF-ih-uh] (probably Philemon's wife) and Archippus [ahr-KIP-uhs] (who may have been his son). The church (probably at Colosse, see Col. 4:9) met in Philemon's house. We are not told how or when Paul met Philemon, but it was probably during Paul's long ministry in and around Ephesus (Acts 19:8-10).

Verses 3-7 show that Paul prayed for Philemon and held him in high regard. He heard reports of Philemon's faith and love. These reports brought Paul great joy. Following these words of greeting and commendation, Paul got around to his reason for writing, beginning in verse 8. He wrote about someone called Onesimus, whom Philemon obviously knew. Paul referred to Onesimus as his **son,** whom he had **begotten in** his **bonds** ("chains," NIV, HCSB, NKJV). **Begotten** means "to cause to be born." This was one way that Paul used to describe those whom he had won to Christ and for whom he felt responsible.

We are told only one thing about the circumstances of their meeting and of Onesimus's conversion. It happened while Paul was imprisoned, probably in Rome. We are not told how or why Onesimus happened to be in Rome or how he came into contact with Paul. He may have met Paul earlier, he may have heard of him and sought him out, or he may have been recognized by some mutual acquaintance and brought to Paul. In any case, the two got together with the result that Onesimus was converted.

Another unknown piece of the puzzle is why Onesimus was in Rome. The general tone of the letter implies that he had run away from

Philemon. He may have stolen from his master (vv. 18-19). Paul called Onesimus formerly **unprofitable** but now potentially **profitable.** Thus he would live up to his name **Onesimus,** which means "profitable" or "useful."

God does not see people as they are but as they can become by His grace. Paul himself was living testimony that God could transform a sinner into a useful servant for the Lord. Paul saw lost people as God sees them and told them of Christ. Then he worked with the new converts to help them see their own potential usefulness to God's kingdom. Paul also challenged others to encourage new converts, immature believers, and straying Christians to fulfill their potential usefulness in the kingdom of God.

Notice the basis for Paul's appeal on behalf of Onesimus. **Wherefore** refers back to Paul's words of praise for Philemon's love and faith in verses 3-7. Based on the kind of person Paul knew Philemon to be, he appealed to his friend. Paul wrote that as an apostle he could have exercised this authority. **Enjoin** is a strong word meaning "command" (NKJV, HCSB) or "order" (NIV). **Convenient** means "what is right, necessary, or proper." In other words Paul told him, "I could be bold and order you to do what you ought to do" (v. 8, NIV). However, although Paul could order Philemon to do what he ought to do, Paul chose to **beseech** ("appeal," NIV, HCSB, NKJV) **for love's sake.** Paul knew that Philemon was a man of faith and love. He also knew how powerful love is as a motivation for Christians.

Paul was not trying to stir Philemon to feel sorry for him, but he did want Philemon to remember that the one who made the appeal was **Paul the aged, and now also a prisoner of Jesus Christ.** "The word which Paul uses of himself is *presbutes,* and Hippocrates, the great Greek medical writer, says that a man is *presbutes,* from the age of forty-nine to the age of fifty-six. Between these years he is what we might call *senior;* only after that does he become a *geron,* which is the Greek for an old man."[1] Paul was reminding Philemon of his credentials as a mature Christian who was imprisoned for his faith. The Letter to Philemon is one of Paul's four Prison Letters, written during his first Roman imprisonment. The others are Philippians, Colossians, and Ephesians. Paul's imprisonment is mentioned several times in this brief letter (vv. 9,10,13,23).

The heart of the appeal in verses 8-11 was for Philemon to realize that Onesimus, who had been useless to him, was now a different man, who would be useful to Philemon. Verse 11 is also the key verse in this lesson on changing our perspective toward another person from someone who is useless to someone who is useful. The lesson could be applied to Onesimus himself, who needed to see himself as a new person in Christ. However, this lesson focuses on Philemon's need to see Onesimus as useful.

Philemon was asked to see his runaway slave as useful not only to him but also to others. How often do people "put down" someone who has not measured up in some way to the expectations of others? "Put down" is only one of many words used to make others feel useless. Others include: "belittle," "berate," "complain," "criticize," "denigrate," "disparage," "mock," "rebuke," "slur," "vilify," and many others. The large number of words shows that humans do a lot of this kind of talk. Physical abuse is terrible, but verbal abuse can also do great damage. Some parents get into the habit of putting down their own children who fail to meet their expectations. Spouses sometimes put down their mates. Some employers do this to their workers. People who constantly are told they are worthless often fulfill such unfair prophecies. The opposite is true of people who learn to affirm and encourage others, even when they fail.

Being useful is more than being utilitarian. When people grow old or sick and are unable to perform the same tasks they once did, they do not cease to be useful and valuable people.

People who are sensitive to others go out of their way to affirm the usefulness and value of those who have meant much to them. A group of men was talking about people in their past who had made a difference for good in their lives. One man paid tribute to a teacher who had helped him when he was a student. This in turn led the man to write a note of appreciation to the elderly teacher, now retired. He received a note from the teacher that said:

> My dear Willie,
>
> I cannot tell you how much your note meant to me. I am in my eighties, living alone in a small room, cooking my own meals, lonely and, like the last leaf of autumn, lingering behind.
>
> You will be interested to know that I taught in school for fifty years and yours is the first note of appreciation I ever received. It came on a blue-cold morning and it cheered me as nothing has in many years.[2]

Valued (Philem. 12-16)

Why did Paul send Onesimus back to Philemon? Was Paul hinting that he expected Philemon to send Onesimus back to help Paul? Why was Onesimus willing to go back? How does verse 15 illustrate Romans 8:28? Was Paul expecting Philemon to set Onesimus free? What is involved in treating others as brothers and sisters in Christ?

Verses 12-14: Whom I have sent again: thou therefore receive him, that is, mine own bowels: [13]whom I would have retained with me, that in thy stead he might have ministered unto me in the bonds of the gospel: [14]but without thy mind would I do nothing; that thy benefit should not be as it were of necessity, but willingly.

Paul wrote Philemon that he had **sent** Onesimus back to him. He sent Onesimus back when he sent the Letter to the Colossians by the hand of Tychicus [TIK-ih-kuhs] (Col. 4:7-9). Apparently Onesimus traveled back to Colosse with Tychicus when he delivered both letters—one to the church and the other to Philemon.

Why did Paul send him back? He did not send him back because he did not care for him, for Paul emphasized in verse 12 how strongly he cared for Onesimus. **Mine own bowels** is confusing language today, but in the first century the inner organs were considered the seat of human emotions. Thus most recent translations use "heart" for **bowels** (NIV, NKJV). Sending Onesimus back was like Paul tearing out his own heart.

Neither did Paul send Onesimus back because he was of no use to him. To the contrary, Paul made it clear Onesimus had been of great help to him. If it were only a matter of Paul's need, he would have **retained** Onesimus to minister to him. As a prisoner, Paul needed helpers. He had some loyal helpers, and Onesimus could have joined those mentioned in verse 24: Mark (Marcus), Luke (Lucas), Aristarchus [ehr-iss-TAHR-kuhs], and Demas.

Paul sent Onesimus back because he was the slave of Philemon, and Paul did not want to make a decision for Philemon. **Without thy mind** means "without your consent" (NIV, HCSB, NKJV). If Paul had made the decision to keep Onesimus, Philemon would have been forced to allow it out of **necessity.** If Philemon made such a decision, Paul wanted it to be **willingly.**

Some Bible students believe Paul's purpose in writing these words was to lead Philemon to send Onesimus back to help Paul. Other Bible students believe Paul's purpose was expressed in verses 11, 16, and 17, not hidden between the lines of verses 13-14.

Verses 15-16: For perhaps he therefore departed for a season, that thou shouldest receive him forever; [16]not now as a servant, but above a servant, a brother beloved, specially to me, but how much more unto thee, both in the flesh, and in the Lord?

Another reason for rejecting the view that Paul's main desire was to have Philemon send Onesimus back to him is that verse 15 says that Paul sent him back to stay with Philemon **forever**. One reason for sending Onesimus was because it seemed to be God's providential plan. Onesimus had **departed for a season, that** Philemon might **receive him forever.** Nothing is said explicitly about God's providence, but that is the idea behind this verse. Onesimus's running away had been an illegal and wrong act, but God had been at work to bring good out of what could have been an even worse situation. This underscores the truth that God sees the potential for good in lost people. Thus God sent Onesimus to where Paul could win him to Christ.

The word **perhaps** reminds us that we do not know why things happen or the good that God can bring out of bad situations. "Paul refers to the separation as though it were God's act, brought about, or at least overruled, by him for the lasting benefit of Philemon and Onesimus alike, and indeed for Paul's benefit too."[3] Richard Melick added: "Onesimus deserved punishment. The grace of God appeared, however, in that Onesimus did not get what he deserved. Rather, his circumstances brought him to a new life. God worked through them to accomplish his purposes *in spite of* failures, misunderstandings, and blatant sins."[4]

Verse 16 is a key verse in determining Paul's purpose for writing. He asked that Philemon receive Onesimus back **as a servant, but above a servant, a brother beloved. Servant** is *doulos,* a "slave," not just a hired servant. Paul made clear that he considered the converted slave **a brother beloved, specially to** him, **but how much more unto** Philemon. Onesimus was now a brother **both in the flesh, and in the Lord**: "He is very dear to me but even dearer to you, both as a man and as a brother in the Lord" (NIV).

In verse 16 Paul went beyond what he indicated to Philemon in verse 11 when he told Philemon he was not just to recognize the new usefulness of the converted runaway to him; he was to receive Onesimus as a Christian brother. That stretched the definition of usefulness beyond mere utility as a slave. Onesimus was now a brother in the Lord whose value as a person extended far beyond his ability and willingness to be a better worker. This concept will transform any relationship.

What was Paul really asking Philemon to do? Was he strongly hinting that Philemon set Onesimus free? Some Bible students think that he was; others doubt that Paul would have asked Philemon to do that. Elsewhere Paul wrote of Christian masters and slaves continuing their status, but having its spirit transformed by the love called for toward brothers and sisters in the Lord. In the flesh, they still were master and slave; but in the Lord, they were brothers in Christ. Of course, the long-range implication of this truth helped to finally bring an end to slavery in Christian lands.

A related question to why Paul sent Onesimus back is why Onesimus voluntarily went back. He must have agreed to go back or Paul could not have sent him back. If Onesimus was not willing, he could have run away from Paul or he could have run away from Tychicus on the long journey from Rome to Colosse. We are not told why Onesimus went back, but the implications are that he went back because being a Christian made him sensitive to the need to ask Philemon for forgiveness and to make a new start. God had used Paul not only to win Onesimus to Christ but also to recognize that he had potential for usefulness in God's kingdom.

The story of Onesimus and Philemon is a case study in the transforming power of the gospel of Christ. The Lord used the witness of Paul to convert a runaway slave. He was so changed that he was willing to go back to his master, even though that was risky. Paul's faith in his Christian brother Philemon led him to trust him to treat his runaway slave as a brother in the Lord.

Earlier we looked at words that devalue people. What are the words that communicate the value that God and Christians see in them? These are words such as "affirm," "commend," "encourage," "forgive," "praise," and others. When we see people only with human eyes, we often fail to see them as God does. He sees each person not as he or she is but as he or she can become by God's grace. Johann von Goethe said, "Treat a man as he appears to be, and you make him worse. But treat a man as if he already were what he potentially could be, and you make him what he should be."[5]

Welcomed (Philem. 17-21)

What makes people partners in Christ? Why is forgiveness costly? Why should Christians give a new start to those who fail? How had Onesimus hurt or taken from Philemon? What did Philemon owe Paul? What more than Paul had asked of Philemon did he expect Philemon to do?

Verses 17-19: **If thou count me therefore a partner, receive him as myself. [18]If he hath wronged thee, or oweth thee ought, put that on mine account; [19]I Paul have written it with mine own hand, I will repay it: albeit I do not say to thee how thou owest unto me even thine own self besides.**

Paul assumed that Philemon counted him to be **a partner.** This word translates *koinonon.* This is from the same root as the more familiar *koinonia,* which refers to the shared life that believers have in Christ. All who belong to Christ are bound together as one. Those who work together for the Lord are **partners.** Paul asked his partner Philemon to **receive** Onesimus **as** he would receive Paul. **Receive** means "welcome" (NIV). The same word is found in Romans 15:7 when Paul called on Jewish and Gentile believers to welcome one another as Christ had welcomed them. Paul expected to be welcomed when he came to the house of Philemon (see v. 22).

Paul used **if** in verse 18 in referring to anything that Onesimus had done to hurt Philemon or to take from him. Any unforgiven hurt or unpaid debt was what Paul meant. He would not have mentioned this if Onesimus had not done something to make himself a debtor to Philemon. The usual assumption is that the slave stole from Philemon as he ran away. Otherwise, how could he have afforded the expenses of the long journey to Rome? But even if Onesimus did not steal, he was robbing Philemon of the work he could have done if he had not left. F. F. Bruce pointed out that the text does not say clearly that the slave had run away. "It could be argued that his master had sent him to fulfill some commission, and that he had overstayed his leave and required a note of excuse from Paul begging pardon for his unduly long absence."[6] This is possible, but most interpreters think the facts favor the view that Onesimus ran away and that he probably stole some money.

Paul said that any debt of Onesimus's should be put **on** his **account.** Of course, Paul had no actual account with Philemon, at least not in the business use of the word. However, Paul was communicating to

Philemon how strongly he felt about the need for Philemon to cancel the debt Onesimus owed. The word *forgive* is not found in this passage, but Paul was talking about forgiveness. To forgive someone is to cancel any debt of pain or loss owed by the offender. Forgiveness is costly because the one forgiving has to absorb the hurt and loss of what the debtor has done.

In passing, Paul reminded Philemon that he owed himself to Paul. This probably means that Paul had been instrumental in Philemon's conversion. When we remember what God and others have paid for our forgiveness, who are we to fail to forgive those who hurt us?

To emphasize this point, Paul himself took the pen in his hand and wrote, **I will repay it.** Ordinarily Paul dictated his letters and someone else acted as his scribe to record his words. But a few times Paul himself wrote some key words for emphasis (see Gal. 6:11).

Verses 20-21: Yea, brother, let me have joy of thee in the Lord: refresh my bowels in the Lord. [21] Having confidence in thy obedience I wrote unto thee, knowing that thou wilt also do more than I say.

Referring to Philemon as **brother,** Paul wrote, **let me have joy of thee in the Lord.** The word translated **joy** is *onaimen.* This word is related to the name Onesimus. It means to have some "benefit" (NIV, NRSV) or "profit." Thus Paul expected to have some benefit from Philemon because of their relationship in the Lord. Paul already had spelled out the benefit he sought in verses 16 and 17. Paul wanted Philemon to welcome Onesimus back as a brother, not just as a slave.

The word **refresh** is the same word Paul used in verse 7, in which he wrote that Philemon refreshed the saints. Paul expressed **confidence in** Philemon's **obedience.** In fact, Paul said that he was confident that his partner and brother would **do more than** Paul asked him to do. Verse 21 raises the question, "What more did Paul expect Philemon to do?" Some Bible students believe this was Paul's way of strongly hinting that he wanted Philemon to set Onesimus free. It may have been, but it also could mean only that Paul expected Philemon to go beyond the letter of the request and welcome Onesimus with the same joy displayed by the father of the prodigal son (Luke 15:11-32).

Another important application of verse 21 is the show of confidence that Paul had in Philemon. He trusted him to do the right thing. Paul could have commanded Philemon, but he chose to trust the love of God at work in and through his friend. This kind of confidence is a strong affirmation of the value of a person. Paul practiced toward

Philemon what he asked the slave owner to do toward his converted slave. He affirmed the usefulness and value of Philemon.

How do you think Philemon responded to Paul's letter? The fact that the early church kept the letter and included it in the books that make up our New Testament is the best evidence that Philemon did what Paul asked him to do.

❖ Spiritual Transformations

Paul witnessed to Onesimus and won him to Christ. He wrote Philemon that his runaway slave was now a Christian and no longer useless but useful. Paul sent Onesimus back and asked Philemon to welcome him as more than a slave—as a Christian brother. He expressed confidence that Philemon would do even more than Paul had asked of him.

Several basic assumptions lie behind this letter:
- God sees people not as they are but as they can become by His grace.
- God uses transformed people such as Paul to win others to Himself.
- God uses people such as Paul to help converts such as Onesimus recognize their potential.
- God uses people such as Paul to appeal to fellow Christians like Philemon to do their part in helping immature believers reach their full potential in Christ.

Who has helped you fulfill your potential as useful in God's kingdom?

_____

How can you help lost people, immature believers, and straying Christians become useful in God's kingdom? _____

_____

Prayer of Commitment: Lord, help me fulfill my maximum usefulness for You, and use me to help others do the same.

[1]William Barclay, *The Letters to Timothy, Titus and Philemon,* second edition, in The Daily Bible Study Series [Philadelphia: The Westminster Press, 1960], 320.

[2]W. E. Sangster, *Sangster's Special-Day Sermons* [Nashville: Abingdon Press, 1960], 147.

[3]F. F. Bruce, *The Epistles to the Colossians, to Philemon, and to the Ephesians,* in The New International Commentary on the New Testament [Grand Rapids: William B. Eerdmans Publishing Company, 1984], 216-217.

[4]Melick, "Philippians, Colossians, Philemon," NAC, 364.

[5]Zuck, *The Speaker's Quote Book,* 291.

[6]F. F. Bruce, *The Epistles to the Colossians, to Philemon, and to the Ephesians,* 197.

DISRESPECT TO RESPECT

Background Passage: 1 Peter 2:13–3:22
Focal Passage: 1 Peter 2:13-21; 3:1-2,7,14-16
Key Verse: 1 Peter 2:17

❖ *Significance of the Lesson*

• The *Theme* of this lesson is that Christ in you moves you from disrespect to respect.
• The *Life Question* is, Why should I respect all people?
• The *Biblical Truth* is that believers are to respect all people and reverence Christ as Lord.
• The *Life Impact* is to help you respect people and reverence Christ.

Disrespect and Respect

In the secular worldview, people may be exploited and belittled. Television characters who show disrespect toward authority figures are viewed as entertaining and funny. People make jokes about their political leaders; steal from their employers; and neglect, mistreat, and even abuse their spouses and children.

In the biblical worldview, all people, especially those in positions of authority or in situations of need, are to be treated with respect and Christ is to be reverenced.

Word Study: *Honor, Fear, and Respect*

The *New International Version* translates two different Greek words (*time* and *phobos*) as "respect" in 1 Peter 2:17,18 and 3:7,15. From this we learn that Christians are obligated to respect authority—be it the governing authorities or those in authority in an employer-employee relationship; respect spouses; and respect those to whom they witness. Christians demonstrate this respect because they reverence Christ as Lord in their hearts. The *King James Version* translates these two Greek words "honor" (2:17; 3:7) and "fear" (2:18; 3:15).

❖ Search the Scriptures

Peter called believers to respect all people, government authorities, and masters. He called Christian wives to live submissive, godly lives to win their husbands; and he called on Christian husbands to treat their wives with respect. He challenged Christians to be ready at all times to give a defense of their hope because they had reverence for Christ.

Respect Authority (1 Pet. 2:13-21)

What words were used to denote respect? How are Christians to think and act toward all people, fellow Christians, government author- ities, God? How were Christian slaves to think and act toward their masters? What applications does this have for modern Christians?

2:13-17: Submit yourselves to every ordinance of man for the Lord's sake: whether it be to the king, as supreme; [14]or unto gov- ernors, as unto them that are sent by him for the punishment of evildoers, and for the praise of them that do well. [15]For so is the will of God, that with well-doing ye may put to silence the igno- rance of foolish men: [16]As free, and not using your liberty for a cloak of maliciousness, but as the servants of God. [17]Honor all men. Love the brotherhood. Fear God. Honor the king.

Four different Greek words were used in these verses to describe some aspect of respect. The first is *hupotagete* in verse 13. When used in the middle voice, it means to "submit yourself" to someone or some- thing. This is the Christian concept of submission; it is voluntary sub- mission. This word is "the translation of a Greek military term meaning 'to arrange in military fashion under the command of a leader.' One could translate, 'put yourselves in the attitude of submission to.' The exhortation is not merely to obey ordinances, but to create and main- tain that attitude of heart which will always lead one to obey them."[1]

In the words **every ordinance of man** the word **ordinance** trans- lates *ktisei.* Because of the mention of government authorities in the same sentence, most translators have assumed that *ktisei* in this pas- sage refers to "every authority instituted among men" (NIV) or "every human institution" (NASB, HCSB). Some Bible students, however, understand the word *ktisei* to mean what it means elsewhere in the New Testament—"creation" or "created being." For example, Peter H. Davids translated it as "every created human being."[2] Since verse 17 calls for believers to **honor all men,** this may be the target group also in verse 13; however, the last part of verse 13 clearly refers to **the king, as supreme,** and verse 14 refers to **governors.**

The king could refer to the Roman emperor, since he was the supreme earthly king in that time. **Governors** were the emperor's representatives in the various parts of the empire. Verses 13-14 and verse 17 mention submitting to the power of the ruling authorities and honoring them appropriately. They also mention the role of the government in punishing **evildoers** and in rewarding those who **do well.**

The kind of persecution when Peter wrote often began with slanderous charges from non-Christians. They accused the believers of all kinds of evils: atheism (because they did not believe in the ancient gods and in the divinity of the emperor), cannibalism (because their critics misunderstood the words spoken at the Lord's Supper), immorality (because of their "love feasts"), and sedition (because they acknowledged Christ as Lord and King). Peter said that by submitting to government authorities the believers would be doing **the will of God,** and they also would **put to silence the ignorance of foolish men.**

Peter did not want his readers to assume that they were to render to Caesar that which is God's—their supreme submission. Therefore, he wrote in verse 16, "Live as free men" (NIV). Yet he did not want them to think that freedom meant liberty to do whatever they desired to do. Therefore, he added **not using your liberty for a cloak of maliciousness** ("cover-up for evil," NIV), **but as the servants of God.** They were not free politically, but they were free in the sight of God; however, this freedom was qualified by their loyalty to God as His servants. They were subjects of the emperor, but they were servants of God.

Verse 17 sums up some key ideas and includes the remaining three words for respect in these verses. They are **honor, love,** and **fear.** The word **honor** is used to describe how they were to respect **all men** and **the king. Love** is used to describe how they were to respect **the brotherhood** ("the brotherhood of believers," NIV). **Fear** was to be given to **God.** Believers are to respect all people in the sense of honoring them. Honor also is due to government officials. A different level of respect is due to Christian brothers and sisters, whom we are to love. We are to fear—give ultimate respect to—God.

Events in the last few decades in our country have led to a mistrust of all institutions, government and its leaders in particular. Many people do not trust the system or respect the leaders. We need to remember that our system with all its human failings is the best system by far in our world today, and we have the responsibility of preserving it and of participating in it. Thomas Jefferson said, "With all the imperfections of our present government, it is without comparison the best existing, or that ever did exist."[3] Our nation has weathered internal disagreements that would have led to armed rebellion in other lands. This shows that a majority of people remains loyal to our country. We may or may not have voted for those in authority, but we have the freedom to vote against them at election time. And while someone is serving in a position of power and responsibility, we are commanded to respect the office.

2:18-21: **Servants, be subject to your masters with all fear; not only to the good and gentle, but also to the froward.** [19]**For this is thankworthy, if a man for conscience toward God endure grief, suffering wrongfully.** [20]**For what glory is it, if, when ye be buffeted for your faults, ye shall take it patiently? but if, when ye do well, and suffer for it, ye take it patiently, this is acceptable with God.** [21]**For even hereunto were ye called: because Christ also suffered for us, leaving us an example, that ye should follow his steps.**

In this passage, Peter addressed **servants** who worked in the household (*oiketai,* from *oikos,* "house"). This would include not only cooks, maids, and other domestic servants but also slaves who served as tutors and nurses for children. Not all slaves were from the lower classes; some were educated foreigners who had been captured in war. Many of the early Christians were slaves; only a few were slave-owners. Philemon was an exception. Paul addressed not only Christian slaves but also Christian masters in Ephesians 6:5-9. By contrast, Peter spoke to Christian slaves whose masters seem to have been non-Christians.

Peter repeated the same word in verse 18 he had used in verse 13. Christian slaves were to **be subject** ("submit yourselves," NIV) to their **masters.** The word for slave owners is *despotais,* from which we get our word *despots.* The masters had total authority over their slaves. The word **fear** also appears in verse 18. Most Bible translations understand the words **with all fear** to refer to fear of their masters. In other words, Peter again was making an appeal for respecting those in authority: "submit yourselves to your masters with all respect" (NIV, HCSB); "be submissive to your masters with all respect" (NASB); "submit to your masters with all due respect" (REB). Peter Davids disagreed. He argued that the word **fear** in 1 Peter always refers to fear of God, not to fear of humans. He wrote: "That this reverence or fear is directed to God, not to masters, is indicated by the facts that (1) the phrase comes before the reference to the masters in the Greek word order, and (2) fear or reverence (Gk. *phobos*) in 1 Peter is always directed toward God, never toward people, whom Christians are *not* to fear (1:17; 2:17; 3:2,6,14,16)."[4]

Some masters were **good and gentle,** but others were **froward** ("harsh," NKJV, NIV, NRSV; "unreasonable," NASB; "cruel," HCSB). Submitting to a kind master was much easier than to a harsh one. Since this letter was written during a time of persecution, non-Christian masters often took out their anger on their slaves who were Christians. Peter's words called on these believing slaves to show by their endurance the reality of their faith.

In verses 19-20 Peter dealt with unjust suffering because of their Christian faith and life. In verse 20 he noted two reasons for a slave to suffer at the hands of a master and commented on each. First, if a slave did wrong, then he had no excuse when he was punished for his wrongdoing, and he should take his just punishment without thinking that it was to his "credit" (NIV, HCSB, NKJV, NASB, NRSV): **For what glory is it, if, when ye be buffeted** ("beaten," NKJV, HCSB) **for your faults, ye shall take it patiently?** But what if the slave was doing good and suffered for it? That situation is what is dealt with in verse 19 and in the last part of verse 20: "But when you do good and suffer, if you take it patiently, this is commendable before God" (NKJV).

In verse 21 Peter gave the highest motivation for patiently enduring unjust punishment. He referred to the unjust suffering of Jesus. Christians are **called** to this way of enduring unjust suffering. This is how Christ suffered. Then in verse 21 Peter made three points about the death of Jesus:

• **Christ also suffered.** Jesus taught that His mission involved suffering. His followers had a hard time accepting this teaching until after the resurrection; then they saw what Jesus had meant.

• **Christ also suffered for us.** Jesus taught that He was suffering for others. Some suffering is the result of living in an imperfect world; some suffering is able to make a person a better person; but the suffering of Jesus was for our salvation. He suffered and died for our sins.

• **Christ also suffered for us, leaving us an example, that ye should follow his steps.** Although Jesus' death was much more than an example, it was also an example for us.

The word **example** "means literally 'writing under.' It was used of words given children to copy, both as a writing exercise and as a means of impressing a moral. Sometimes it was used with reference to the act of tracing over written letters."[5] Christ is first of all our Savior, but He then becomes our example. We **should follow his steps.** This is not possible for anyone except by the power of the crucified and risen Lord working in and through their lives.

The context of 1 Peter 2:21 was the need for Christian slaves to endure unjust suffering because their Lord had endured unjust suffering on their behalf. They should be ready to follow Him in the way of the cross. This principle, however, applies to all believers today. We are to follow the example of our Lord by following in His steps.

We no longer have slavery in this country, but some of the principles Peter wrote to Christian slaves apply to work settings in our day. One is that employees and employers owe each other respect. Another is that Christian workers or managers ought to live a Christian life in the workplace. Inconsistent living by professing Christians has a negative effect of non-Christians with whom the inconsistent Christians live and work. Consistent living can be used by the Lord to win others to salvation.

Respect Spouses (1 Pet. 3:1-2,7)

How are Christian wives to show respect for their husbands? What if the husband is not a believer? How are Christian husbands to show respect for their wives? How can a Christian couple show mutual respect?

3:1-2: Likewise ye wives, be in subjection to your own husbands; that, if any obey not the word, they also may without the word be won by the conversation of the wives; ²while they behold your chaste conversation coupled with fear.

These verses deal with the respect to be shown by Christian wives who had non-Christian husbands. Since believers were taught to marry only believers, most of these situations were when the wife of a non-Christian marriage became a Christian but the husband did not.

Likewise points back to the principle of humble submission and respect for all people (2:13,17). It does not mean that a wife is the slave of her husband. **Be in subjection** is the same word that is used in 2:13 of submission to government leaders and in 2:18 of slaves to their masters. As we have noted already, the words **be in subjection** refer to the voluntary submission of Christian wives to their husbands, not to the husbands subjecting their wives to themselves. Paul used the same word in Ephesians 5:24 and Colossians 3:18 for the submission of Christian wives to their husbands. The difference may be that Paul was assuming an ideal description of marriage in which a Christian husband loved his wife and gave himself for her. Peter was writing to situations where the husband was unsaved. In either case, Christian wives are called on to submit themselves to their husbands.

In reference to **husbands,** when Peter wrote **if any obey not the word,** the word translated **obey not** "means literally in its verb form, 'not to allow one's self to be persuaded.' These husbands were of that obstinate, non-persuadable type that will not listen to reason. Their wives had often given them the gospel, but they had met it with stiff-necked obstinacy."[6] Although the wife was to voluntarily submit to her husband, she was not expected to give up her faith because her husband told her to do so. Instead, she should do what she could to see him **won.** This word meant "acquire" or "gain, but in Christian use it referred to conversion to Christ.

What was a Christian wife to do to win her husband who already had heard and rejected **the word** ("the Christian message," HCSB)? Peter called on the Christian wife to do three things. First of all, she was to live in humble submission to her husband insofar as it did not involve renouncing her faith. In other words, she was to win him by how she lived. The word translated **conversation** refers to more than what is said; it refers to one's whole way of life ("behavior," NIV, NASB; "conduct," NRSV; "the way their wives live," HCSB). In fact, **without the word** means "without saying anything to him." The unbelieving husband already had heard "the Christian message" (HCSB); now what he needed was to see Christ in the way his wife lived day by day. Second, her way of life was also to be **chaste.** She was to be unquestionably faithful or "pure" (HCSB). Third, the Christian wife was to demonstrate her **fear** or reverence of God.

3:7: Likewise, ye husbands, dwell with them according to knowledge, giving honor unto the wife, as unto the weaker vessel, and as being heirs together of the grace of life; that your prayers be not hindered.

This verse was addressed to Christian husbands. This is the only time the word translated **dwell with** is used in the New Testament. It appears eight times, however, in the Septuagint (the Greek translation of the Old Testament), where it often included living together in sexual oneness. The word thus indicates that a Christian husband is to be faithful to his lifetime commitment to his wife. **Knowledge** has the ideas of understanding and consideration involved in it. Christian husbands are to see things from the point of view of their wives, not just from their own perspective.

Christian husbands were to give **honor unto the wife, as unto the weaker vessel.** This use of **weaker** refers only to physical strength, not to moral, spiritual, or intellectual weakness. **Honor** means to recognize and affirm her value and worth. Another word for this is "respect" (NIV, REB).

The last part of verse 7 adds further positive aspects of a Christian marriage. Although the wife is to recognize the leadership role of her husband, the husband should recognize that the two of them are **heirs together of the grace of life.** There is no hint of any spiritual inferiority. Both are joint heirs of the same grace of God. Peter emphasized this so **that** their **prayers be not hindered.** These words stress the spiritual foundation of Christian marriage. In a Christian marriage, both husband and wife are to be committed to the same God of grace. Prayer is to be the foundation for their marriage.

What is involved in showing respect for one's spouse in Christian marriage? One thing it means is avoiding anything that shows disrespect for one's spouse. A Christian marriage is based on a lifetime commitment to each other and to the Lord. Any enduring marriage passes through many stages as a couple matures. In today's world, one non-Christian assumption of many people is that the purpose of life is for each person to find happiness on his or her own terms. Many married people use this as a reason for destroying their marriage in the self-centered search for happiness and fulfillment. Those who look toward the needs of the other spouse ride out the rough spots in marriage because they show respect and love for each other.

Reverence Christ (1 Pet. 3:14-16)

What responses to unjust treatment should Christians make? How should these responses be made? What is the desired result of these responses?

3:14-16: **But and if ye suffer for righteousness' sake, happy are ye: and be not afraid of their terror, neither be troubled; [15]but sanctify the Lord God in your hearts: and be ready always to give an answer to every man that asketh you a reason of the hope that is in**

you with meekness and fear: [16]having a good conscience; that, whereas they speak evil of you, as of evildoers, they may be ashamed that falsely accuse your good conversation in Christ.

Peter had just written that in a just society, good people should have nothing to fear (v. 13). In verse 14, he dealt with how to respond if they were called on to **suffer for righteousness' sake.** This was one of Jesus' Beatitudes (Matt. 5:10-12). Peter, like Jesus, pronounced such people as **happy** (the same word as "blessed") those who do this. Then Peter summarized Isaiah 8:12-13, saying, **Be not afraid of their terror, neither be troubled.** Thus the first two responses are to be willing to suffer for righteousness' sake and not to fear the ones who threaten.

Peter concentrated on the third response, however: **Sanctify the Lord God in your hearts.** Many ancient copies of 1 Peter have "sanctify Christ as Lord in your hearts" (NASB, and similarly in other versions). **Sanctify** means to "set apart" (NIV, HCSB). The word has two ideas: reverence for Christ and commitment to Him. Most of verses 15-16 describe how to do this.

In the words **be ready always to give an answer to every man that asketh you a reason for the hope that is in you,** the key word is **answer,** *apologian.* This word was used for the defense made in a courtroom or an explanation given for one's actions. It may have referred to either in verse 16. We get our English word *apology* from it. In theology, an apology is not an expression of regret but an explanation of our faith to those who call it in question, an *apologia.* Those who are skilled at doing this we call *apologists.* The non-Christian world of the first century was raising questions and making false charges against the life and beliefs of Christians. Peter said that each believer needed to **be ready always** to respond to such challenges, seeing these as opportunities to bear testimony to our **hope** in Christ. In our day this calls for some Christians to be Christian apologists, who present the intellectual basis for our faith and thus help all Christians be able to tell others why they are Christians.

This witnessing is to be done **with meekness** ("humility" or "gentleness," NIV, HCSB, NASB, NRSV) **and fear** ("respect," NIV, HCSB). The words **with meekness and fear** have two possible interpretations. It is possible that both terms refer to the attitude that believers are to have toward others. Christians are to be meek and respect those to whom they witness. Or, it may be that the first term **(meekness)** refers to the attitude Christians are to have toward others in witnessing and the second term **(fear)** refers to their attitude toward God ("reverence," NASB, NRSV).

Slandered Christians should have **a good conscience** because the charges against them were false. They were not **evildoers** as their persecutors charged. The hoped-for result of this approach was that the persecutors and critics would **be ashamed** because their slanders proved to be unfounded. The godly way of life (**good conversation,** as in v. 1) of believers could have such an effect.

❖ *Spiritual Transformations*

Several forms of showing respect for others are as follows: (1) Submit to the authority of government leaders, masters (employers), and husbands. (2) Honor government leaders, all people, and wives. (3) Love fellow Christians, spouses, and seek to win unsaved husbands and persecutors to the Lord. (4) Reverence Christ as Lord by telling the lost the reasons we are Christians, enduring unjust suffering, living a consistent Christian life, having a Christian marriage, and praying.

Respecting other people has several levels, depending on the person or group. On the basic level we ought to respect all people as fellow human beings. We ought to acknowledge the authority of those in positions of authority. We ought to show tender mutual respect for our spouses. And we ought to respect those to whom we share the good news of Jesus Christ. This respect for others grows out of our reverence for the Lord.

In what specific relations do you need to show greater respect to others? _____

In what ways do you need to show greater reverence for Christ?
_____

Prayer of Commitment: Lord, help me show deep reverence for You and proper respect for others.

[1]Kenneth S. Wuest, *First Peter in the Greek New Testament,* in Wuest's Word Studies [Grand Rapids: William B. Eerdmans Publishing Company, 1942], 60.

[2]Peter H. Davids, *The First Epistle of Peter,* in The New International Commentary on the New Testament [Grand Rapids: William B. Eerdmans Publishing Company, 1990], 98.

[3]Carruth and Ehrlich, *American Quotations,* 255.

[4]Peter Davids, *The First Epistle of Peter,* 106.

[5]Wuest, *First Peter,* 67.

[6]Wuest. *First Peter,* 72.

PREJUDICE TO ACCEPTANCE

Bible Passage: James 2:1-13
Key Verse: James 2:1

❖ *Significance of the Lesson*

• The *Theme* of this lesson is that Christ in you moves you from prejudice to acceptance.

• The *Life Question* this lesson challenges us with is, Am I prejudiced against others?

• The *Biblical Truth* is that prejudice is sin.

• The *Life Impact* is to help you overcome your prejudices and to resist prejudices where you find them.

Worldviews About Prejudice

In the secular worldview, people often prejudge others by outward appearances. People are accepted or rejected based on economic status, social standing, and race. Prejudice sometimes infects even the church. In some churches poor people or people of different races are either rejected or ignored. "Good prospects" often are defined as those most like the church members, especially if their wealth or prestige can enhance the wealth or prestige of the church.

In the biblical worldview, God deals with all people fairly without regard for outward appearances or the group to which they belong. Prejudice is sin. True followers of the Lord Jesus are to show His kind of compassion for all people.

Word Study: *Respect of persons*

The Greek word James used in 2:1,9 literally means "to lift up the face." It is a compound word combining the words for "face" and "receive." The origin of this word reflects the practice of ancient kings to lift up the down-turned faces of people in the king's presence. "To lift up one's face" was a sign of favor by the king. Thus the word came to refer to showing favoritism or partiality to someone. It is the opposite of being impartial and treating everyone alike.

The Old Testament said that God does not show respect of persons; in other words, He is impartial (2 Chron. 19:5-7). He called His people to be impartial (Lev. 19:15; Deut.1:17). This same message is delivered in the New Testament. Jesus was impartial (Luke 20:21). Peter declared that God is no respecter of persons (Acts 10:34). Paul announced the same truth in Romans 2:11. Christians are warned against this sin (Eph. 6:9; Col. 3:25). The English words *prejudice, partiality, favoritism* best represent this idea. *Prejudice* is prejudging others on the basis of outward appearances. It is showing favor or lack of favor to people based on this standard.

❖ *Search the Scriptures*

After warning of the sin of prejudice, James gave an example of a rich man being welcomed and a poor man being shunned when they visited the church. By doing this, the believers despised the poor whom God has chosen and fawned over the rich, who exploited and persecuted the believers. James called for following the royal law of love for one's neighbor. He warned believers they will be judged based on the law of liberty.

Denouncing Favoritism (Jas. 2:1-4)

*Why is **respect of persons** inconsistent with faith in the Lord Jesus Christ? To what other prejudices does this principle apply? What words describe the two visitors who came to the church? How was each treated and why? How serious is the sin of partiality? How would these two kinds of visitors be received in your church?* These questions are addressed in comments on these verses.

Verse 1: My brethren, have not the faith of our Lord Jesus Christ, the Lord of glory, with respect of persons.

This is a hard verse to translate. Literally, it says, "Not in partiality hold the faith of our Lord Jesus Christ of glory." Did James mean this to be a command or a question? Some translations see it as a question: "Do you with your acts of favoritism really believe in our glorious Lord Jesus Christ?" (NRSV). Most translations see it as a command: "Do not hold the faith of our Lord Jesus Christ, the Lord of glory, with partiality" (NKJV); "Hold your faith in our glorious Lord Jesus Christ without showing favoritism" (HCSB). What is meant by **the faith of our Lord Jesus Christ**? This is what it called an objective genitive. It can be translated "faith in" (NASB, HCSB). What is the impact of the words **the Lord of glory**? The idea seems to be the biblical teaching that the glory of God is revealed in Jesus Christ. Since God shows no favoritism, neither should those who have faith in Christ.

On the surface, English readers of the *King James Version* today might think the words **respect of persons** refer to respecting other people; and they may wonder why believers are not to do this. However, as we saw in the "Word Study," the Greek word means "partiality," "favoritism," or "prejudice." Thus the point of this verse is that partiality is inconsistent with faith in the One who is gracious and fair in His dealings with all kinds of people and has no partiality. In Greek the word is plural. Thus it seems to refer to all kinds of prejudices, not just the one dealt with in verses 2-3. Included would be prejudices based on race, education, social status, or any other. Any prejudice is inconsistent with faith in the Lord Jesus. Showing prejudice is a mark of empty religion, not of the true faith in Jesus Christ.

Verses 2-4: **For if there come unto your assembly a man with a gold ring, in goodly apparel, and there come in also a poor man in vile raiment; [3]and ye have respect to him that weareth the gay clothing, and say unto him, Sit thou here in a good place; and say to the poor, Stand thou there, or sit here under my footstool: [4]Are ye not then partial in yourselves, and are become judges of evil thoughts?**

Having stated the basic principle, James gave a practical example of what he meant. **Assembly** is the word *synagogue.* The word here, however, probably was used in its generic sense of a meeting of Christians. The two who came seem to have been visitors, not regular members. James painted a vivid contrast between the two men. One was **a man with a gold ring, in goodly apparel. Gold ring** is a word that means literally "a gold-fingered man." This was a mark of wealth and prestige, much as a person today with expensive rings, jewelry, and a watch. Very likely, the man flaunted his ring or rings. The word **goodly** in **goodly apparel** translates *lampra*, which means "bright," "shining," "splendid," or "fine."

The other man was **poor.** James used *ptochos*, the word for abject poverty. He had on **vile raiment** ("filthy clothes," NKJV; "shabby clothes," NIV; "dirty clothes," NASB, NRSV, HCSB). This poor man was at the other end of the economic and social scale from the rich man.

The ushers and leaders of the church treated each man differently. They were profuse in their welcome to the rich man, saying, **Sit thou here in a good place.** They bent over backward to welcome him and give him a place of honor. However, they told the poor man, **Stand thou there, or sit here under my footstool.** We have little knowledge of the seating arrangements in the early assemblies, which often met in homes. **Under my footstool** may mean "Sit on the floor by my feet" (NIV) or "Sit here on the floor by my footstool" (HCSB). They tried to get the poor man out of the way and put him in a place where he would not be seen.

Verse 4 is God's condemnation of those who commit the sin of partiality. **Partial in yourselves** can mean "discriminated among yourselves" (NIV, HCSB) or it could refer to their own inner division of heart that was in back of such discrimination toward others. **Judges of evil thoughts** can mean "judges with evil thoughts" (NIV, HCSB, NRSV) or "judges with evil motives" (NASB). Verse 4 reinforces the idea in verse 1 by condemning partiality.

What is human partiality or prejudice? Isn't it making distinctions between people based only on outward appearances? Humans tend to judge and prejudge people based on what they can see. By contrast, God looks on the heart. Only He has the knowledge and character to act as judge. Prejudice excludes or despises those whose appearance is against them or who belong to a group who are considered worthless or enemies.

Before we judge these ancients too strongly, we need to ask ourselves how these same two visitors would be treated in our churches today. Would they be treated any differently than they were then? Every generation seems to consider rich people to be the brightest and best of society. In our day, this includes rich and famous entertainers, athletes, and entrepreneurs.

Often worship of the outwardly successful carries over into the church. When a rich or famous person visits most modern congregations, people roll out the red carpet. Like those in James's time, we fawn over such people. We covet them for our church, thinking what new wealth and prestige they would bring with them. At the same time, we seldom seek those who are destitute or poor. When by chance one of them shows up, dressed as was the man in James, many churches fail to make the person welcome and may even shun him.

Seeing Through God's Eyes (Jas. 2:5-7)

In what sense might it be said that God has a bias toward the poor? How serious was the sinful way this congregation had treated the poor man? In what ways did the rich of that day harm believers and their cause?

Verses 5-7: Hearken, my beloved brethren, Hath not God chosen the poor of this world rich in faith, and heirs of the kingdom which he hath promised to them that love him? ⁶But ye have despised the poor. Do not rich men oppress you, and draw you before the judgment seats? ⁷Do not they blaspheme that worthy name by the which ye are called?

Hearken was a call to pay careful attention to what James was about to write. He began by reminding them that if God has a bias at all, it is in favor of **the poor of this world.** It is true that God is impartial, but He gives special attention to the needs of those who are so often oppressed by others. **God** has **chosen the poor of this world** to be **rich in faith, and heirs of the kingdom which he hath promised to them that love him.** This does not mean that God does not also call the rich to come unto Him. But those who are rich often are too preoccupied with their earthly possessions to be concerned about laying up treasures for the eternal kingdom. Their wealth is their god and their ultimate trust. The poor in this world's goods more easily recognize their need for God.

Yet these poor people whom God loves and calls, this church had **despised** ("insulted" NIV; "dishonored," NRSV, NASB, NKJV, HCSB). Their shunning of the poor visitor was an insult to the man. Put yourself in his place. How would you have felt at such treatment in the house of God? Would you likely return and expose yourself to such shabby treatment again? His clothes may have been shabby, but their treatment of him was more shabby. This strong language shows how seriously God considers the sin of prejudice toward any person of any group.

When members of another race attended some churches during the days of the civil rights movement, some church members said: "They are just testing us. They didn't really come to worship." Other members wondered, "If we were being tested, did we pass or fail the test from the viewpoint of our Heavenly Father? How many people do we normally ask at the door, 'Have you come to truly worship?'" If we asked such a question, and people gave honest answers, how many would be able to answer Yes?

James asked two rhetorical questions. First, he reminded them that **rich men** oppressed them and dragged them into court **(before the judgment seats).** Second, he reminded them that the rich blasphemed the **worthy name by which** they were **called.** In other words, the rich and powerful of that day were among those who persecuted Christians. Yet when a rich man visited the church, the people went out of their way to make him welcome. Welcoming a visitor is a good thing to do, but welcoming only the rich and despising the poor is a serious sin.

The title of this lesson is "Prejudice to Acceptance." What kind of acceptance is proper? Doesn't it mean that we welcome to our assembly any visitor? Doesn't it also mean that we welcome into the church as a first-class member anyone who has a genuine experience with Jesus Christ regardless of his or her social-economic status or race? In the early churches, Jewish Christians sometimes failed to do this with Gentile converts and vice-versa. Paul had this in mind when he wrote, "Receive ye one another, as Christ also received us to the glory of God" (Rom. 15:7).

Verses 6-7 show two troubling consequences of prejudice. On the one hand, prejudice excludes and even shames some people. On the other hand, it blinds us to the faults of those whom we favor based on outward things. These consequences grow out of the nature of prejudice. On the one hand, it is blind to the faults of some groups and to the virtues of the others. Members of one group make certain assumptions about all members of the other group. For example, some say, "Those street people are all just a bunch of lazy dead-beats who wouldn't work if they had a chance to do so." This is sometimes called "stereotyping" or "the lumping fallacy." Assumptions are made about all members of a group, based on observation or reports of a few. None of us want to be judged by the worst people in our group.

Living by the Royal Law (Jas. 2:8-11)

What is **the** *royal law? How does it relate to the sin of prejudice? How serious is this sin?*

Verse 8: **If ye fulfill the royal law according to the scripture, Thou shalt love thy neighbor as thyself, ye do well.**

The royal law is, **Thou shalt love thy neighbor as thyself.** This is found in Leviticus 19:18, and it is quoted by Jesus as the second part of the love commandment (Matt. 22:35-40). It fulfills all the Ten Commandments having to do with human relations (Rom. 13:8-10).

Loving your neighbor is the antidote for the sin of partiality. Three facts about this are important to notice:

1. Love involves doing good for your neighbor. Those who do good for others will not despise them or exclude them, but will welcome and care for them.

2. All people are our neighbors. No person or group is excluded from the circle of our responsibility.

3. Our love for our neighbors is based on God's love for all of us. It does not start with love of self but with God's love for each of us and for all of us.

Verses 9-11: **But if ye have respect to persons, ye commit sin, and are convinced of the law as transgressors.** [10]**For whosoever shall keep the whole law, and yet offend in one point, he is guilty of all.** [11]**For he that said, Do not commit adultery, said also, Do not kill. Now if thou commit no adultery, yet if thou kill, thou art become a transgressor of the law.**

James warned, **If ye have respect to persons, ye commit sin.** They were condemned by **the royal law,** which they had broken. The law of God is like a mirror. One strong blow and it shatters. Verse 10 may sound unfair, but keep in mind that the law is a fabric that sets forth the will of God. Breaking the law of love for neighbor involves many other sins as well. The examples in verse 11 are of serious sins, and partiality or prejudice is a serious sin.

The Bible offers many examples of prejudice and the evil consequences that followed. The Israelites hated and feared the Assyrians so much that Jonah did his best to avoid going to them with the call to repentance. Then when he obeyed and they repented, Jonah pouted because God showed mercy to these enemies of his nation (Jon. 4). In New Testament times, the Jews and Samaritans had such hostility between them that one Samaritan village forbade Jesus to enter, and James and John wanted to call down fire from heaven on the hated Samaritans (Luke 9:52-56). Prejudice between Jews and Gentiles kept the Jerusalem believers from obeying the Great

Commission. Peter himself had to be led step by step to recognize that God is impartial and wants to offer His love for Gentiles (Acts 10). Much of the evil in the world has its roots in partiality or prejudice. Prejudice has spawned violence, wars, and even genocide. And prejudice has kept Christian people from offering Christ's love to countless people and from welcoming those who do receive Christ. True believers in Jesus Christ are to live by the royal law and love others as they do themselves.

Facing God's Judgment (Jas. 2:12-13)

*What is **the law of liberty**? Who will be judged by it? On what basis will be the judgment? How will **mercy** rejoice against **judgment**?*

Verses 12-13: So speak ye, and so do, as they that shall be judged by the law of liberty. [13]For he shall have judgment without mercy, that hath showed no mercy; and mercy rejoiceth against judgment.

The law of liberty is probably another way of describing the Word of God with its message of good news of deliverance and freedom from sin and death. The good news is both a gift from God and a demand for faith and obedience when we receive it. Paul said that believers are free from the demands of the law as a way for seeking God's favor (Gal. 5:1), but they are bound by the higher demands of Christian love and the leadership of God's Spirit (vv. 13,16-25). The law of love for neighbor is a part of the demand of love and the Spirit. We are to **speak** and **do** ("act," NIV, HCSB), **as they that shall be judged by the law of liberty.** Although believers have been saved by grace and have assurance of eternal life, we are still subject to divine judgments in life and beyond. "For we must all appear before the judgment seat of Christ; that every one may receive the things done in his body, according to that he hath done, whether it be good or bad" (2 Cor. 5:10). One area this judgment will deal with is how we treated people who were different from us and our group. Sins of partiality and prejudice will be judged.

God is impartial in His role of Savior, and He is also impartial in His role as Judge. He will judge according to truth and reality. His **judgment** will be **without mercy** on people who **showed no mercy.** This teaching is similar to the parable of the unforgiving servant in Matthew 18:21-35. Those who have truly received the mercy of God will be merciful to others. Failing to show mercy to others raises doubts about our own forgiveness. Forgiveness and love are two-way streets of the heart. Hearts that are open to receive God's mercy will allow that mercy to flow out to others. If the flow is blocked in one way, it is blocked in both ways. The criteria by which we judge and prejudge others will be applied to us.

But for those who demonstrate they have received God's mercy by showing mercy to others, **mercy rejoiceth against judgment**— or "mercy triumphs over judgment" (NIV, HCSB). Mercy wins a double victory—in our hearts and in the lives of those whom we have loved in Jesus' name.

❖ *Spiritual Transformations*

This lesson's Bible content teaches four basic truths about prejudice:
- Prejudice is inconsistent with the Christian faith.
- Prejudice mistreats those whom God loves.
- Prejudice is a sin against the royal law of love for one's neighbor.
- Prejudice is an unmerciful act for which people will be judged.

Prejudice is a sensitive subject. Many people deny they are prejudiced. They, therefore, resent anyone confronting them with the sin of prejudice. However, the Bible speaks clearly about this sin and calls us to the way of impartial love for all people. In the early 1970s there were some Bible studies in our Southern Baptist Sunday School curriculum on some controversial issues of that day. The objective was to see what the Bible said about poverty, race, war and peace, and alcohol. Letting God's Word speak to them and seeking to obey it changed some people. Not everyone responded positively. One Sunday School teacher reported that someone said: "I don't care what the Bible says about this. I know how I feel about it, and I don't intend to change." Do *you* ever feel this way?

What kinds of prejudices are most prevalent today in the area where you live? _____

What would you say is your greatest prejudice? _____
_____

How have you let and how are you letting the Lord help you over-come personal prejudices? _____

Prayer of Commitment: Forgive me, Lord, for my sins of prejudice; and help me to show Your kind of love to all others.

COVETING TO CONTENTMENT

Background Passage: Romans 7:7-11; Philippians 4:10-19;
1 Timothy 6:6-10
**Focal Passage: Romans 7:7-8; Philippians 4:10-13;
1 Timothy 6:6-10**
Key Verse: 1 Timothy 6:6

❖ *Significance of the Lesson*

• The *Theme* of this lesson is that Christ in you moves you from coveting to contentment.
• The *Life Question* this lesson seeks to address is, Am I content with what I have?
• The *Biblical Truth* is that contentment comes from Christ.
• The *Life Impact* is to help you find your contentment in Christ.

Contentment and Discontentment

In the secular worldview, wants are confused with needs. Many adults are discontented because they don't have all the things they want. Influenced by the commercials they see on television, some adults want every new creature comfort. Many adults go into debt to maintain a standard of living that "keeps up with the Joneses."

In the biblical worldview, material possessions are not the source of contentment. Contentment comes from focusing on the eternal and trusting Christ to supply life's needs.

Word Study: *Content, Contentment*

The Stoic philosophers used the words *content* and *contentment* to describe the kind of contentment and self-sufficiency they sought. Paul used the word "content" in Philippians 4:11 and the word "contentment" in 1 Timothy 6:6 to refer to being content in Christ. Paul's contentment, however, was not the self-sufficiency of the Stoics but the sufficiency found in Christ.

❖ *Search the Scriptures*

The sin of covetousness is illustrated by the fact that the law not only defined sin but also led to the very sins that it forbade. For example, the Tenth Commandment not only made people aware of the sin of covetousness but also stirred up their sinful natures to covet. The secret of contentment is illustrated by Paul's unusual expression of thanks to the Philippians. He was more grateful for their giving than for the gift because he had learned to be content with what he had. The seduction of riches is illustrated in Paul's warning about the dangers of the love of money. He commended the kind of godliness that is of greater value than material wealth.

The Sin of Covetousness (Rom. 7:7-8)

How does the law make people aware of sin? How does it stir people to commit the sins forbidden by the law? Why are people lured by forbidden fruit? What is the sin of covetousness? What is distinctive about the Tenth Commandment? These questions are addressed in comments on these verses.

Romans 7:7-8: What shall we say then? Is the law sin? God forbid. Nay, I had not known sin, but by the law: for I had not known lust, except the law had said, Thou shalt not covet. [8]But sin, taking occasion by the commandment, wrought in me all manner of concupiscence. For without the law sin was dead.

Verses 7-8 make two main points: The law defines what sin is, and the law provokes people to sin.

Paul strongly denied he was saying that the law itself is sinful. He asked, **Is the law sin?** His quick answer was, **God forbid** ("Certainly not!" NIV, NKJV; "Absolutely not!" HCSB). However, Paul wrote that he would **not** have **known sin, but by the law.** He gave an example of how the Tenth Commandment, **Thou shalt not covet,** had led him to know **lust** ("covetousness," NKJV). **Covet** is *epithumeseis*. **Lust** is the noun form of the same root word (*epithumian*). This word means "desires." In the New Testament it usually is used of sinful desires and often of sexual lusts; however, it can refer to desires in general. Here it refers to the desires that lead to transgressions of the Tenth Commandment.

Verse 8 takes the argument one step further. Not only does the Tenth Commandment define covetousness and forbid it, but it also stirs up in people **all manner of concupiscence** (this is same word translated **lust** in v. 7). This is not the fault of the commandment itself but of **sin**. Paul stated that **sin, taking occasion by the commandment, wrought in** him all kinds of desires. **Occasion** means "opportunity." **Wrought** means "produced." Hence, "But sin, taking opportunity by the commandment, produced in me all manner of evil desire" (NKJV). Paul ended verse 8 by saying, **For without the law sin was dead.**

The earliest and best illustration of this in Scripture is the lure of the forbidden fruit in Genesis 2–3. The tempter used the one prohibition God gave Adam and Eve to lure them into eating the forbidden fruit. Something about human nature causes us to be lured by the very things that God forbids.

In his *Confessions*, Saint Augustine told of an experience from his youth. Near his home was an orchard laden with fruit. He and his friends were tempted to steal the fruit. Years later he confessed: "We carried away thence huge burdens of fruit, not for our own eating but to be cast before the hogs; and, if we did taste thereof at all, it was not for any reason so much as because we would do that which is was not lawful."[1]

Paul referred to the Tenth Commandment, which forbids coveting. What is *covetousness*? Isn't it a mixture of greed and envy? *Greed* is the insatiable desire for more and more material things for ourselves. *Envy* is wanting what others have. Put them together and you have covetousness. The Tenth Commandment forbids coveting anything that belongs to a neighbor.

This commandment is distinctive since most of the others, especially the Sixth through the Ninth, relate to specific acts: murder, adultery, stealing, and slander. Jesus led us to look behind these to see the inner motivation (see Matt. 5:21-22,27-28). But the Tenth Commandment from the beginning dealt with an inner attitude. Coveting cannot be seen until it leads to action; however, it is sin even as an attitude. Is it any wonder Jesus said, "Take heed, and beware of covetousness: for a man's life consisteth not in the abundance of the things which he possesseth" (Luke 12:15)?

The Secret of Contentment (Phil. 4:10-13)

In what ways is this passage an unusual expression of thanks to the Philippians for a gift? Why were the Philippians slow to send the gift?

How did Paul's view of contentment differ from the Stoics' view? What was the secret of Paul's contentment? Why is such contentment so rare?

Philippians 4:10-13: But I rejoiced in the Lord greatly, that now at the last your care of me hath flourished again; wherein ye were also careful, but ye lacked opportunity. [11]Not that I speak in respect of want: for I have learned, in whatsoever state I am, therewith to be content. [12]I know both how to be abased, and I know how to abound: everywhere and in all things I am instructed both to be full and to be hungry, both to abound and to suffer need. [13]I can do all things through Christ which stengtheneth me.

Verses 10-13 are Paul's expression of thanks for the gift sent to him by the Philippian church. They had sent money and one of their own members to minister to the apostle (2:25-30; 4:15-19). However, this is one of the most unusual thank-you notes of all time. For one thing, Paul waited until near the end of the letter to thank them. Why? He may have already written to thank them. More likely, the reasons are threefold. First, he was more grateful for the givers than for the gifts. Paul began and ended his Letter to the Philippians by expressing thanks for them. Second, he made clear that he did not have to receive their gifts. Third, his primary purposes in writing were other than thanking them for their gifts. For example, he was concerned with the potential for dissension in their church.

Another unusual thing is that Paul seems to have begun verse 10 with a complaint that they had taken so long to send their offering. He began with the familiar, **I rejoiced in the Lord greatly**; but then he added, **that now at the last your care of me hath flourished again** ("at last you have renewed your concern for me," NIV). However, Paul quickly tried to correct any misunderstanding of what he meant. He was not complaining that they had deliberately failed to send help to him. He wrote that he realized that it was not that they did not care about him; the problem was that they **lacked opportunity.** Paul did not explain what he meant. Perhaps the Philippians had not heard for a long time of Paul's imprisonment. It took a long time for news to travel from Rome to Philippi and then for someone to journey back with an offering for Paul. At any rate, Paul was not complaining about the delay. Two things make this clear: For one thing, verses 11-12 make plain that he did not need the gift. And for another thing, he later expressed loving gratitude for the Philippians (see vv. 15-20).

In verse 11 Paul emphasized that he was not writing out of deep **want**: "I am not saying this because I am in need" (NIV). The word **want** (*husteresin*) refers to deep need (the verb form of this word occurs at the end of verse 12). Paul explained, **I have learned, in whatsoever state I am, therewith to be content. Content** (*autarkes*) was a key word used by Stoic philosophers in Paul's day. They used it to mean "self-sufficient." By that they meant not "that one is oblivious to circumstances, but that the truly *autarkes* person is not determined by such. One is 'independent' of others and of circumstances in the sense of being free from their either causing distress or effecting serenity. Serenity comes from being sufficient unto oneself."[2] The secret of Paul's sufficiency, however, was not in himself but in Christ. As he stated in verse 13, **I can do all things through Christ which stengtheneth me.**

Paul spelled out his contentment in verse 12: **I know both how to be abased, and I know how to abound. Abased** means "to be humbled" or "to be brought low." **I am instructed** is the Greek word *memuemai*, a word used by the first-century mystery religions to mean "I found the secret." Hence the *New International Version*'s rendering, "I have learned the secret of being content in any and every situation." Paul was content whether he was **full** or **hungry** ("whether well fed or hungry," NIV). He had learned **both to abound and to suffer need.**

Abound translates *perisseuein* twice in verse 12. Later in the chapter Paul used the same word when he wrote, "I have all, and abound" (v. 18). Imagine a person in Paul's circumstances writing such a thing! He was under house arrest awaiting trial, yet he maintained a joy and peace in the Lord. He could do this because he felt he was in the center of the Lord's will doing what the Lord would have him to do. And he trusted the Lord to supply all he needed to continue to do that.

What was Paul's secret of contentment? In a word, Christ. Trusting Christ and depending on Him for all he needed was Paul's secret of contentment. Paul's testimony was: **I can do all things through Christ which stengtheneth me.**

Paul's testimony is remarkable because such contentment is so rare. In fact, most people are the exact opposite of Paul. He was contented with material things, but he was constantly seeking to become better in moral and spiritual things (3:12-14). Most people are content or complacent about their moral and spiritual progress, but they are continually discontented with their material possessions. They have not learned the true secret of contentment.

The Seduction of Riches (1 Tim. 6:6-10)

*What kind of **gain** comes from **godliness**? How does the truth in verse 7 motivate a right view of possessions? How does the truth in verse 8 reflect the teachings of Jesus in Matthew 6:25-34? Do Paul's teachings undermine ambition and the free enterprise system? How can believers decide when they have enough? What are some common misunderstandings of verse 10a? Why is **the love of money** such a strong temptation? What are some of the evil consequences of the love of money?*

1 Timothy 6:6-8: But godliness with contentment is great gain. ⁷For we brought nothing into this world, and it is certain we can carry nothing out. ⁸And having food and raiment let us be therewith content.

In 1 Timothy 6:5 Paul warned against false teachers who taught that "gain is godliness" ("who think that godliness is a means to financial gain," NIV). In other words, they were teaching that religious devotion and godly living lead to material gain. This teaching is still set forth by some today. They promise material blessings to those who do right. Paul warned believers to turn away from such teachings.

Instead, Paul used the same words in verse 6 to teach that **godliness with contentment is great gain.** The differences in wording between verses 5 and 6 are the addition of **with contentment** and **great.** Paul believed that **great** spiritual blessings come to those who live reverent and godly lives. **Godliness** means to be reverent toward God and to live in light of that reverence. **Contentment** is a form of the same word Paul used in Philippians 4:11. **Gain** describes a means of obtaining material things.

In verse 7 Paul gave a reason for godly living and contentment with what one has. A similar proverbial saying to verse 7 is found in the literature of many cultures. It is something that everyone knows to be true but that many ignore. Job said, "Naked came I out of my mother's womb, and naked shall I return thither" (Job 1:21). The modern proverb is "You can't take it with you." We take out of the world the same thing with which we entered the world—**nothing.** You probably have heard the story of two friends at the lavish funeral of a rich man.

One asked, "How much did he leave?" The other answered, "He left it all." Since this is true, only shortsighted people live only to accumulate what they leave behind. Jesus contrasted treasures on earth, which are insecure and earthbound, with treasures in heaven, which are secure and eternal (Matt. 6:19-21).

Verse 8, **and having food and raiment let us be therewith content,** reminds us of Philippians 4:12, and both remind us of Matthew 6: 25-34. Jesus warned against anxiety about food and clothing. He showed that such anxiety is useless and dangerous. Instead, he called for trust in the heavenly Father and concentration on the kingdom of God. **Be . . . content** translates a passive verb that means "to have enough" or "to be content with what one has."

1 Timothy 6:9-10: **But they that will be rich fall into temptation and a snare, and into many foolish and hurtful lusts, which drown men in destruction and perdition. ¹⁰For the love of money is the root of all evil: which while some coveted after, they have erred from the faith, and pierced themselves through with many sorrows.**

In verses 9-10 Paul addressed **they that will be rich. Will be** refers to "those who desire to be rich" (NKJV) or "people who want to get rich" (NIV). He warned them that **the love of money is the root of all evil.** And he spoke about some of the evil consequences those who **coveted after** money have experienced. The word translated **coveted after** literally means "to stretch oneself "or "to reach out one's hand for something." Figuratively it means "aspire to," "strive for," or "to desire." Thus it can be translated "reaching for" (NEB), "longing for" (NASB), "in pursuit of " (REB), "by craving" (HCSB), or "eager for" (NIV).

Augustine perceptively wrote: "It is not a matter of possession but of desire. One man may have much money on him but no greed in him, whereas another may have no money on him but much greed in him."[3]

The first part of verse 10 is the most familiar part of the passage, but it is often misquoted to say that money itself is the root of all evil. The Bible never says that money is the root of all evil; it says that **the love of money is the root of all evil.** The word for **root** has no definite article before it. Thus many see it as referring to "a root" (NIV, HCSB, NKJV, NRSV). **Of all evil** means "of all kinds of evil" (NIV, HCSB, NKJV, NRSV). Paul was not saying that the love of money is the one root of every kind of evil. Thus two common *misunderstandings* of this verse are (1) that it teaches that *money itself* is evil, and (2) that it teaches that the love of money is *the cause* of all evil. Not all sins come from the love of money—but many do. We would have a long list if we could name all the evils for which the love of money is a primary cause. These would include robbery, gambling, dishonesty, leaving God out, exploitation of others, and so on.

The last parts of verses 9-10 describe the consequences of seeking to become rich. Those who do **fall into temptation and a snare** ("trap," NIV, HCSB). The seduction of riches is a powerful temptation, and it often leads people to yield to the temptation; and when they do, they fall into a trap. They also fall into **many foolish and hurtful lusts. Lusts** refers to all kinds of evil desires. These prove to be **foolish** in the long run because sin is basically irrational. They are also **hurtful** ("harmful," NIV, HCSB, NKJV). In addition, these evil desires **drown men in destruction and perdition** ("ruin and destruction," NIV, HCSB, NRSV, NASB). **Drown** refers to sinking to the bottom. Thus Paul warned of the three steps to ruin from covetousness: Being tempted, being snared, and being destroyed. At the end of verse 10 Paul stated that some who covet after money **have erred from the faith, and pierced themselves through with many sorrows.**

Someone may ask: "Was Paul opposed to ambition, and are his teachings contrary to the free enterprise system?" Paul was not denying legitimate ambition, but he was warning that ambition for money could easily get out of hand. Ambition is out of hand when it becomes selfish and when it consumes our time and energy so that we neglect our relationship with God and others, especially our families. Making a living is a legitimate Christian action, in fact a duty (see 5:8). Supplying the needs of our families is important. Earning money to have something to give to the needy is also a Christian ambition (Eph. 4:28). If you have nothing of your own, you have nothing to give.

Most of us struggle with the question of how much is enough for the legitimate needs of our families, for gifts to others, and for reasonable security against misfortune. We live in a society that continually moves our *wants* to the list of things we think we *need*. Actually humans have few basic needs. In the first century many believers were concerned primarily about survival. The same was true in our land during the Great Depression. Having food, clothing, and shelter were the goals. During times of prosperity, people assume that they have these basic needs; so they concentrate on things they want. The advertising industry is constantly influencing people to move things out of the wants column to the needs column. This results in the kind of discontentment that blights many lives and feeds the desire for riches. Many people—including many Christian people—need to move from covetousness to contentment.

❖ *Spiritual Transformations*

In Romans 7:7-8 Paul described how the law brought an awareness of what sin is and also stirred up the very sins that it forbade. He applied this to the Tenth Commandment. He testified in Philippians 4:10-13 to how he had learned the secret of being contented with little or with much. In 1 Timothy 6:6-10 Paul warned against the dangers of striving to be rich.

This lesson is right on target for our society. The world's striving for more and more things tempts Christians. Covetousness blights the lives of many people, including some believers. Learning to practice gratitude and contentment is not an easy discipline in a society that defines many wants as needs. The secret Paul has shown to us is to find our sufficiency in Christ, not in things. This involves commitment to Him and trust in Him to supply all that we need as we seek to do the will of God.

What wants have you moved to needs? _____

_____

What steps do you commit to take to have contentment in Christ and not in earthly possessions and things? _____

_____

Prayer of Commitment: Lord, help me to find the contentment that comes when You are my sufficiency. Amen.

[1]Augustine, *The Confessions of St. Augustine* [London: Fontana Books, 1963]. 62.
[2]Fee, *Paul's Letter to the Philippians*, 432.
[3]Quoted in Zuck, *The Speaker's Quote Book*, 179.

STOCKPILING TO SHARING

Bible Passage: Luke 12:13-21; 21:1-4
Key Verse: Luke 12:15

❖ *Significance of the Lesson*

• The *Theme* of this lesson is that Christ in you moves you from stockpiling to sharing.
• The *Life Question* this lesson seeks to address is, What should I do with what I have?
• The *Biblical Truth* is that being rich toward God is more important than accumulating material possessions.
• The *Life Impact* is to help you be a sharing person.

Attitudes Toward Sharing

In the secular worldview, a person cannot have too many possessions. Status is determined and success is judged by the size of one's house, the amount of one's income and worth, and the number of one's possessions. Sharing with others has low priority.

In the biblical worldview, life is more than material possessions. How one uses possessions is important. Living in relationship with God and sharing with others are more important than accumulating things.

Relation to the Previous Lesson

The lessons for February 17 and 24 are similar. Both condemn greed and covetousness. However, the previous lesson's positive emphasis was *contentment* while this lesson focuses on *sharing*. These two Christian responses to material things are complementary. That is, people who are content with what they have are more likely to share with others. Another difference is that in the first lesson one person—Paul—is the one who moved from covetousness to contentment. In this lesson, two people—the man in Luke 12:13-15 and the rich farmer—represent stockpiling, while a different person—the poor widow—represents sharing.

Word Study: *Covetousness*

Two New Testament Greek words can be translated *covetousness* or *covet*. One is *epithumia*, which Paul used in Romans 7:7 in reference to what he discovered about himself in light of the Tenth Commandment. That verb means "to have a desire." A second word is *pleonexia*; this is the word in Luke 12:15. The word means "the desire for more and more." Many newer translations use "greed" to translate this word into English. *Covetousness* and *greed* are often used as synonyms in English, but *covetousness* adds envy to greed.

❖ *Search the Scriptures*

When a man asked Jesus to tell his brother to divide the inheritance with him, Jesus warned everyone about the danger of greed, saying that life is more than possessions. He then told the parable of the rich fool to illustrate the dangers of preoccupation with material possessions. Later in His ministry, Jesus commended the poor widow who gave to God all she had.

Guard Against Greed (Luke 12:13-15)

What did the man from the crowd ask Jesus to do? Did the man have a legitimate grievance? Why did Jesus refuse to intervene? What lesson did He draw from this request? To whom did He address His warning? Why is verse 15 so needed today?

12:13-15: And one of the company said unto him, Master, speak to my brother, that he divide the inheritance with me. ¹⁴And he said unto him, Man, who made me a judge or a divider over you? ¹⁵And he said unto them, Take heed, and beware of covetousness: for a man's life consisteth not in the abundance of the things which he possesseth.

Some of Jesus' most important actions and teachings came after He was asked a question or received a request. While He was teaching, **one of the company** ("someone in the crowd," NIV) suddenly asked Jesus to do something for him. He wanted Jesus to **speak to** his **brother, that he divide the inheritance with** him ("tell my brother to divide the inheritance with me," NIV). This man's name is not given. He just suddenly emerged from the crowd and made this request.

The Old Testament law said that if there were two brothers, the older would receive twice as much of the inheritance as the younger (Deut. 21:15-17). We assume that this man was the younger brother. Had his older brother refused to share his portion with him? Many Bible students believe that this was the situation. Others, however, believe that the man wanted more than the law allowed him. The basis for this view is Jesus' warning about **covetousness.** They ask, "Why would Jesus warn him against greed unless the man was seeking more than he was due?" The former group, however, notes that the warning of verse 15 was addressed to more than this one man. Actually, we do not know the exact situation. All we know is what the Bible tells us. The man asked Jesus to tell his brother to **divide the inheritance** with him. Notice that he did not ask Jesus to mediate the dispute. He asked Him to tell his brother to do this.

We also know that Jesus refused to act as **a judge or a divider** ("arbitrator," NKJV, HCSB, NASB, NRSV; "arbiter," NIV) in this situation. He called Jesus **Master** ("Teacher," NIV), a title of respect. The man knew that Jewish rabbis sometimes helped to resolve differences growing out of different understandings of the law. Jesus' address to him, **Man,** is a term of rebuke. By His response, Jesus was not indicating that He never acted as a judge but that He chose not to do so here. He sensed something wrong about the man's attitude toward possessions.

Jesus' warning in verse 15 was addressed not only to this man but also to everyone, no doubt including the man's brother. Indeed, if the older brother was cheating his younger brother, he certainly needed to hear what Jesus said in verse 15. **Take heed, and beware** ("Watch out! Be on your guard against," NIV) introduces a warning that all people need to hear. Jesus' warning was against **covetousness** ("all kinds of greed," NIV), which literally means "the desire for more and more." Paul identified this sin as idolatry in Ephesians 5:5 and Colossians 3:5. It is making a god of possessions by becoming preoccupied with getting, having, and enjoying possessions for oneself.

Jesus' reason for warning against greed was that **a man's life consisteth not in the abundance of the things which he possesseth.** The *New English Bible* reads, "Even when a man has more than enough, his wealth does not give him life." **Life** is *zoe*, the higher life that has potential for relating to God and others. Greed consumes people so much that they miss the real purpose for life. Their idea of real living and of the good life is defined by how many possessions they have.

Vance Packard in his book *The Waste Makers* pointed to the spreading materialism of modern society. He dedicated the book with this inscription: "To my mother and father, who have never confused the possession of goods with the good life."[1]

Jesus' saying is a clear denial of a basic assumption of a secular worldview. Because believers live in a society in which wealth is identified with life, we are tempted to adopt the secular view as our own. People think, *If I just had plenty of money, I could really begin to live.* Abundant possessions are the standard of success by which most people judge themselves and others. People who are rich consider themselves secure and successful. Others also consider them the same way. Jesus warned that those who have this attitude are not secure or successful; to the contrary, they have missed what life is all about.

All the pressures of our culture move us toward this identification of possessions with life. Television commercials picture the good life in terms of the abundance of possessions. This error is not a modern phenomenon. The Roman writer Horace wrote, "Get money by fair means if you can; if not, get money."[2] A modern example of this advice is that given by one father to his son: "Son, make money. If you can, make money honestly. But if you can't make money honestly, my son, I still want you to make money!"[3]

Gain Spiritual Riches (Luke 12:16-21)

*Was this man condemned for being rich, for having a good crop, or for planning for the future? Was he condemned for dishonesty, for exploitation, or for laziness? What is the surprise element in the parable? How did he plan to handle the problem of storing his abundant harvest? What is the significance of his repeated use of I and **my**? What were his long-range plans for his own future? Why did God call this man a **fool**? What is involved in being rich toward God? How should the man have responded to his abundant harvest? How does this parable illustrate verse 15?*

12:16-21: And he spake a parable unto them, saying, The ground of a certain rich man brought forth plentifully: [17]and he thought within himself, saying, What shall I do, because I have no room where to bestow my fruits? [18]And he said, This will I do: I will pull down my barns, and build greater; and there will I bestow all my fruits and my goods. [19]And I will say to my soul, Soul, thou hast

much goods laid up for many years; take thine ease, eat, drink, and be merry. ²⁰But God said unto him, Thou fool, this night thy soul shall be required of thee: then whose shall those things be, which thou hast provided? ²¹So is he that layeth up treasure for himself, and is not rich toward God.

In response to this incident and to illustrate the saying in verse 15, Jesus told them **a parable.** The parables of Jesus often were illustrations taken from ordinary, daily living; but they often had some twist or surprise to make His point. This parable was about **a certain rich man.** Notice that the man already was rich before the events in the story. Apparently this was not the first time **the ground . . . brought forth plentifully** for this rich man, but this bountiful harvest presented a problem since it was more than he had **room** to store in his current buildings.

As the rich farmer considered his options, **he said, This will I do: I will pull down my barns, and build greater.** This action would provide space for him to store all his **fruits** and his **goods.** We learn later in the story that all of this was only in the planning stage. It never happened because the man died that night. However, dying was the furthest thing from his mind as he planned for his short-range and long-range future. Verse 19 gives his long-range plan. After he had finished his project, he anticipated a retirement that would be both secure and enjoyable. Notice the wording: **I will say to my soul, Soul, thou hast much goods laid up for many years; take thine ease, eat, drink, and be merry.**

Several things are worthy of note in these words: The rich man assumed he had plenty of possessions—enough to provide for a secure future. He also assumed he had many years to enjoy them. His words at the end of verse 19 were a familiar saying. Those who planned to live in sinful and sensual indulgence often used this saying. This may have been what the farmer meant. He had been a hard-working farmer; perhaps he intended to live in the fast lane after he retired. On the other hand, he may have meant only that he intended to enjoy a life of leisure, free from the pressures of daily work.

The word translated **soul** is *psyche*, which also appears in verse 20. The meaning in verse 19 is probably not intended to refer to his eternal soul so much as to himself. The *New International Version* and the *Holman Christian Standard Bible* both introduce the verse with the words: "I'll say to myself."

The surprise in the parable for the man and for the people who heard Jesus tell the parable comes in verses 20-21. **God** called the man a **fool.** As far as the average person was concerned, the man seemed a model of what all desired. Why would God call him a fool? Let's look back over the parable and see why God called him a fool.

God did not accuse the rich man of some of the sins elsewhere condemned in wealthy people. For example, there is no hint that the man had gotten his wealth by being dishonest. Nor was he accused of exploiting those who worked for him. And he surely was not a thief who used violence to get his money. No, there is every reason to believe that the man was an honest, hardworking farmer. Why then was he called a fool?

First of all, there is no mention of any relationship to God or concern for others. How would a person of faith and love respond to the bountiful harvest? For one thing, a believer would thank God for these blessings. The man was so self-centered and preoccupied with his possessions that he had no time for God. A person with love in his heart would also be thinking of the opportunities for helping others that came with his new prosperity. Instead of thanking God and sharing with others, the man took personal credit for his good crop. Notice the repetition of the words **I** and **my** in verses 17-19. He considered himself and his hard work the reasons for the good harvest. By ignoring the needs of others, the man became guilty of the sin of selfishness and indifference to the needs of others.

Another foolish thing he did was to assume he could buy security with money; and closely related was his assumption he would live forever. Wealth is never secure. We may speak of financial security, but Jesus warned that earthly treasures are subject to all kinds of hazards: "Lay not up for yourselves treasures upon earth, where moth and rust doth corrupt, and where thieves break through and steal" (Matt. 6:19). Of course, the ultimate folly of the mirage of financial security is the shortness and uncertainty of life. James 4:13-16 is a warning to business people against presuming they will be here tomorrow and the next day to continue to buy and sell. The rich farmer discovered the danger of such presumption, but he found it too late to help him.

When God confronted him on the night of his death, He asked him, **Whose shall those things be, which thou hast provided?** We are not told who inherited what he had called his barns and his crops. The question emphasizes that the one thing for sure was they were no longer his. He should have realized that much earlier. None of us owns what we call our own. We only have the use of our possessions for a limited time. All things belong to God, and we are to be good stewards of what is His.

Jesus stated the lesson of the parable in verse 21. The goal of life is to be **rich toward God.** From a negative point of view, this means that we will not become preoccupied with laying up treasure for ourselves on earth. To do so is deadly.

Tolstoy told of a man who was promised that he would have for his own all the land that he could walk around between sunrise and sunset. He got an early start and walked with confidence that, by the end of the day, he would be the owner of a vast estate. As he walked, he kept extending the boundaries of what he wanted. The farther he went, the faster he walked. He burned with fever, but one word drove him on—"more." He threw off his shirt and boots. He felt his heart beating like a drum, but he forced himself to go on. Just as the sun set, he threw himself forward as he reached out for the goal. And as he did, he dropped dead. But he got his land—for they took a shovel and gave him a strip of soil six by two.[4]

From a positive point of view, it means to have a right relation with God and others. Dr. Walter Judd planned to follow God's call as a medical missionary. When he graduated from medical school, one of his professors chided him for wasting his life in this way. When Dr. Judd was on furlough, he visited his alma mater; and that same professor sought him out. "You remember, Judd, how I advised you against going to the Orient. I'm not so sure now. Take my own life for instance. As a young man I had four major ambitions, all of which have been realized. First, I wanted to be the best possible doctor I was capable of becoming. Second, I wanted to be a doctor's doctor, a man other medical men would seek when they needed attention. . . . Third, I wanted an income so I could have a home with the appointments my family could enjoy. . . . Fourth, I wanted a fine wife and children. . . . But Dr. Judd, I feel as if all these things are slipping through my fingers. What's wrong with my life?"

Dr. Judd was kind enough not to speak the truth to his old professor. But in his heart he was saying: "Sir, there is nothing wrong in the four ambitions you set for your life. The only difficulty is that they all revolved around you and your family. You did not go far enough in your dreams, and now you are seeing the truth of Jesus' warning that those who think they can find their lives and order them to their own interests eventually will lose them."[5]

Give Sacrificially (Luke 21:1-4)

Where did this event take place? Why did the poor widow give all she had? Why did Jesus say that she gave more than all the others? Does God expect us to give all we have?

21:1-4: And he looked up, and saw the rich men casting their gifts into the treasury. [2]And he saw also a certain poor widow casting in thither two mites. [3]And he said, Of a truth I say unto you, that this poor widow hath cast in more than they all: [4]For all these have of their abundance cast in unto the offerings of God: but she of her penury hath cast in all the living that she had.

Treasury ("temple treasury," NIV, HCSB) translates *gazophulakion*, which were 13 trumpet-shaped receptacles in the Court of the Women in the temple—an "offering box" (CEV). People put their gifts in these for the purpose of temple expenses. Jesus **looked up** because Mark 12:41 states He was sitting and watching people bringing their offerings. He **saw the rich men casting their gifts into the treasury.** Mark noted, "Many that were rich cast in much" (v. 41).

Jesus **saw also a certain poor widow casting in thither two mites. Mites,** *leptas,* were coins of the smallest value. Two words for **poor** describe the woman. In verse 2 she is called *penichran*, which "refers to someone who is needy or poor. . . . It can be an intensive term: the 'very poor.'"[6] In verse 3 she is called *ptoche*, a more common word for poor.

Of a truth I say unto you alerts us to something of special note that Jesus is about to say. He said that her small gift was **more than** all the others had given. Obviously it was not of greater monetary value, but Jesus considered it more. He explained why in verse 4. The rich gave out **of their abundance.** But **she of her penury hath cast in all the living that she had. Penury** is an old word that means "poverty" (NIV, HCSB, NKJV). **Living** translates *bios*, which refers here to her "means of living"—"all she had to live on" (NIV, HCSB, NRSV). No one can give more than that.

Robert H. Stein listed four lessons based on this incident: "(1) the measure of one's gift does not involve how much one gives but how much remains, that is, how much one keeps; (2) a gift is measured by the spirit in which it is given; (3) one's giving should be commensurate with one's means; and (4) true giving involves giving all one has."[7]

George Mueller said, "God judges what we give by what we keep."[8] The wealthy men brought rich gifts, but they probably did not really miss what they gave because they had so much left to use for themselves. But the widow had nothing left to live on. Hers was truly a sacrifice.

Does God expect us to give Him all that we have? Jesus told the rich young ruler to sell all that he had and give it to the poor. He did this because the man had placed his trust in his riches (18:18-24). The Lord does not ask each of us to do that, but He does ask that we place at His disposal ourselves and all we have (Rom. 12:1; 2 Cor. 8:5). Many people give nothing to the Lord or to others (Luke 12:16-21; 16:19-31). Others give only the leftovers (Mal. 1:13). Some—like the rich in Luke 21:1—give large amounts, but they never give so much that they really miss it.

Herschel H. Hobbs told of commending a man for a large gift, but the man said: "Pastor, I do not deserve your commendation. For it involved no sacrifice on my part. During this year I have worn fine clothes, lived in a fine house, eaten good food, bought my wife a new car, and have taken her on a trip to Europe. I have deprived myself of nothing. There are many people who have given more than I have. Perhaps it is some poor widow who gave a much smaller amount but at a greater sacrifice."[9]

God rejoices over sacrificial giving. This is the kind of giving Christ Himself did. Paul commended the Macedonian believers for sacrificial giving (2 Cor. 8:2). Then he showed how such giving reflected Jesus' giving: "For ye know the grace of our Lord Jesus Christ, that, though he was rich, yet for your sakes he became poor, that ye through his poverty might be rich" (v. 9).

This lesson is about moving from stockpiling to sharing. This is how contentment relates to sacrificial giving. Stockpiling is storing up for possible future needs. There is a difference between reasonable saving for the future and stockpiling. Stockpiling and never sharing is sinful. It shows a lack of faith, love, and contentment. Many people in our society are like the rich farmer in Luke 12:16-21. They devote most of their time and energy to laying up wealth. Too many people have allowed themselves to get caught up in maintaining a higher standard of living than they need. Thus they never seem to have enough for the present or to store up enough for maintaining their desired standard of living. Those who live with gratitude and contentment learn that they do not need as much for themselves and also learn to trust God to provide for their present and future needs.

Sacrificial giving expresses great devotion to God, contentment with what God has given, and strong trust in Him to provide for future needs. In nearly every church there are members who are no longer able to attend church, but some of these people regularly send in their tithes and offerings to the church. Often these are people on small, fixed incomes. They are like the widow of Luke 21:1-4.

❖ *Spiritual Transformations*

Jesus warned against greed after the man asked Jesus to tell his brother to divide the inheritance with him. Jesus told the parable of the rich fool to illustrate the danger of riches on earth with no riches in heaven. The example of the poor widow who gave all she had shows the importance of sacrificial giving.

Are you a giving person? Have you learned that life is for giving? Are you giving in a generous and sacrificial way? _____
_____

How do you decide what you should save for future needs and how much to give to help others with immediate needs? _____
_____

How do you use limited resources in doing your part to meet the seemingly limitless needs of our world? _____
_____

Prayer of Commitment: Lord, You taught that it is more blessed to give than to receive. Help me to live by that rule.

---

[1]Quoted by Wallace Denton, *What's Happening to Our Families* [Philadelphia: The Westminster Press, 1963], 132.

[2]Quoted in *Dictionary of Quotations*, edited by Bergen Evans [New York: Avenel Books, 1978], 461.

[3]Robert J. Hastings, *My Money and God* [Nashville: Broadman Press, 1961], 22.

[4]J. Wallace Hamilton, *Ride the Wild Horses!* [Westwood, NJ: Fleming H. Revell Company, 1952], 54.

[5]Hastings, *My Money and God*, 38-39.

[6]Darrell L. Bock, *Luke 9:51–24:53*, in Baker Exegetical Commentary on the New Testament, vol. 3b (Grand Rapids: Baker Book House, 1996], 1645.

[7]Stein, "Luke," NAC, 508.

[8]Quoted in Zuck, *The Speaker's Quote Book*, 163.

[9]Herschel H. Hobbs, *An Exposition of the Gospel of Luke*, 291.

批社会各界的朋友,他们多年来热心于发展湖湘文化,作者从他们那里得到和引证的资料文章众多,限于篇幅和联系困难,未能与这些资料文章的作者取得联系,笔者对他们的学术贡献深表敬意,对于未能联系到的资料作者,我们将按规定支付稿费和资料费,请致电 010—68408032 与我们联系。

周兴旺

鸣　谢

　　著名经济学家、教育家茅于轼先生审读了本书并亲笔题词，著名政治评论家、人民日报评论员马立诚先生抱病审读本书并命笔谬赞，著名文化评论家、原中国社科院研究员黎鸣先生审读本书并为本书作序，著名政治学者、社会学家周鸿陵先生多次与作者探讨学理并为本书撰写评论，著名记者、工人日报湖南记者站站长方大丰先生多次为本书提出批评建议并奉献采访心得，著名管理评论学者、北京兆维集团总裁办公室主任王家彬先生为本书担任经济顾问并多次主持咨询讨论会。笔者对上述专家学者对我这部作品给予的宝贵支持和批评表示衷心的谢意。

　　新华出版社的领导和编辑对本书非常重视，多次提出修正意见，他们严谨的编辑态度和对人文作品的器重让人感动。人民日报社记者王建新对作者的创作鼎力相助，北京百思达文化公司赵向东、赵向阳先生不辞辛劳，全力支持本书的创作出版，北京朗博广告公司的设计专家申占君、李炜、李昊翰为本书提供了精美新颖的设计方案。作者对他们的辛勤劳动和支持安慰表示感谢。

　　中央文献研究室的专家审读了本书，并对本书出版给予了大力支持。

　　本书参考引证了大量的文献文章资料，其中徐焰先生、周秋光先生、朱汉民先生、易中天先生、傅国涌先生、刘健安先生、谭小平先生等专家学者的研究成果对本书贡献巨大，此外还有大果哪位读者有心购买本书,还请看得清楚明白,千万别存心成全盗版商人,毕竟本书作者不是有钱人,而且作者索要的稿费很低廉,为的是不把本书的价格抬上去;如果哪级文化出版管理部门发现本书的盗版赝品,请务必出重手查缴打击,千万别对不法书贩睁只眼闭只眼,因为那些人最伤文人们的心。

　　所有这些,都是希望列位理解文人的困境和难处,别让与我遭遇近似的酸臭文人流血又流泪。

　　就此打住吧!

周兴旺

2002 年 8 月于北京

不被朝廷看好，却偏偏身在草野心在郢都，最终落了个费力不讨好的下场。著名的贾谊也差不多，满朝文武都不看好这个年纪小口气大的酸秀才，最终也落了个伤心而死的归宿。即使到了近代，魏源、郭嵩焘的下场也没好到哪里去。

这种酸臭的脾气到了当代，依然被湖南人所继承，在全民经商的时代，湖南人却扛起了搞文化的旗帜。我常常奇怪，经济上并不阔绰的湖南卫视为什么要花大价钱投拍"千年论坛"，而著名的《到北大听讲座》的策划制作，也竟然出自几个湖南打工者的手笔。

湖南人的这种流传千年的酸臭文人梦，真的还没有做够吗？

季羡林先生曾经感叹：中国的知识分子好像是特殊材料做成的，要求人的甚少，给予人的甚多，即使是备受委屈，却依然不改自己那片初衷，这是怎样的一群中国人？

季老先生可谓中国文人的知心人，倘若国人对自己的文人多一点宽容，多一点理解和支持，文人们干得就会更欢，产量就会更高，国家就会更发达，百姓的生活就会更红火。对此，你信不信？

又说回来，笔者在这里大肆标榜文人气，还捎带一点私心，就是希望列位看官谅解文人的这种臭脾气，如果本书触动了尊驾的哪根敏感神经，引起您的不快，就请您看在文人的酸劲上，付之一笑即可，千万别动肝火；如果哪位评论家看着本书不顺眼，也千万别无限地上纲上线，给作者戴高帽子，请您看在文人的臭性情上，能放一马就放一马；如果哪位盗版商家看上了本书，那就求你良心发现，大发慈悲，看在文人十年寒窗含辛茹苦以至于写得吐血的可怜份上，高抬贵手，别再打本书的主意；如网络则自认是个文科生，伺候高科技不是咱的特长。如果安心写点畅销书，那也不失为一条终南捷径，可偏偏又不是主持人，至于拍写真，就凭自己这副尊容，那就自己留着敝帚自珍吧。

《湖南人，凭什么》是一本文人书，不是说它文化味有多浓厚，而是指它是我这个酸臭文人用典型的文人脾气腌制出来的。

这本书前后算起来，花了我10年时间，那时候我还是个大学生，每次经过长沙，总是有事没事要到岳麓书院周遭去转悠一通，我常常慨叹：岳麓山并不高，为什么能有幸埋忠骨？岳麓书院不大，为什么代代出雄才？

探悉湖南人的成材秘诀的欲望，大概从这个时候就开始了吧。

后来到北京的报社做了记者，每年都要到湖南采访探亲，写了不少批评老乡的报道，从内心深处，又感到愧对父老乡亲，可是湖南的发展的确不尽如人意，眼瞧着在全国的棋盘上，湘字号不断地黯淡，文人的那种"哀其不幸，怒其不争"的酸臭脾气又发作了，总是觉得不给自己的父老乡亲想出点法子，就愧对他们的养育之恩。

到老家投资办厂力有不济，回老家当个公仆又没有路径，于是发下宏愿，要写出一本书，把湖南人的光荣昭告天下，邀集天下有识之士，为湖南人开单子，出药方。这也是我写本书的一桩心愿。

为了创作本书，我单薄的身体又瘦了几斤，已经记不清多少个夜晚，我挑灯夜战，夜以继日，至于蓬头垢面、形影相吊、惹烦邻居、聒噪家人更是不用提了。

湖南曾经是酸臭文人的老家所在。著名的屈原，明明已经曾有过从政的机会，我没有接受，也曾有过发财的路子，我偏偏拒绝，就是做个记者嘛，现在也有不少发财出名的门道，可我偏偏没有做成这类风光的记者，至今只能当个小记者，每天忙着涂涂改改，同窗都已经是主任记者或者是部主任、副总编什么的，我的名片上的头衔还是记者而已。你说不是酸，是什么？

我从小身材奇瘦，刚刚一米七的个子，是名副其实的小个子，却偏偏喜欢说大话，经常操闲心，虽然屡次被人教诲"不通世故"却依然故我。微薄的工资大多用来买了书，虽知道稿费钱还抵不过买书钱，却仍然醉心于写点东西，每当写到得意之处，就血压升高瞳孔放大，其自我满足之状，就是换个神仙皇帝，也不愿意做了。

我的这种自恋的臭脾气，自然招不来什么好运气。领导说我是典型的眼高手低型，志大才疏，自然不加青睐。而女同志又认为我形象不佳，加之囊中羞涩，自然难以垂青。

于是，一半是自愿，一半是无奈，我便专心做起了职业文人的行当。

有人认为文人其实也很有"钱途"，我的朋友就曾提出过笔杆子里面出金钱的；理论，文人可以炒股、炒楼花、搞策划、弄网络、做咨询，哪样不来钱呢？即使不幸做了文字匠，只要邀得美女作家或者无耻文人的雅号，多到电视台亮亮相，时不时弄出点绯闻趣事来，也不愁销路啊。要不，为什么那些主持人或者影视明星出的自传书和写真集，比陈寅恪、钱钟书他们的作品效益要好多了呢？

可是自己总觉得脑子里仿佛缺根弦，炒股总是看年报，结果买谁的被谁蒙，看楼看广告，从来没有遇上货真价实的，搞策划总是跟老板鼓吹诚信为先的道理，结果总是第一批被人轰走，弄

后　记
文人心　报国情

后记通常是作者向读者汇报自己的创作体会，我也不免要落入这个俗套，自我表白一番。

我总觉得，在中国，做什么职业都挺好，就是做文人不太好。

做文人，总是带股酸臭味。

说文人酸，就是指文人喜欢瞎操心，身无半文，却偏偏喜欢心忧天下，而且常常喜欢找这个时代的毛病，尽拣人家不爱听的说，有时候明知道人家不爱听，还得千方百计塞到人家耳朵里去。说得好听一点，像牛虻，能够督促老牛清醒，说得不好听一点，像蚊蝇，总是在人家耳边骚扰，打搅人家的清梦。言不及义，大而不当，吃着咸菜操心淡汤，不是酸是什么。

说文人臭，就是指文人喜欢臭美，没钱没势没地位，却偏偏喜欢摆弄自己那几把刷子，躲在小房子里皓首穷经，苦思冥想，搜肠刮肚，写出点文章诗歌什么的，又偏偏渴望别人欣赏，最好是引起别人的击节称赏，如果能够被大方之家采纳付诸实行那就更好了。

所以，自古以来文人的社会形象就不太好。

可我自己觉得，我走的大概就是这类酸臭文人的路子。也